T0356492

THE
FORGOTTEN
DECADE

THE FORGOTTEN DECADE

Compelling Stories of the
1970s Cleveland Browns

Roger Gordon

THE FORGOTTEN DECADE
COMPELLING STORIES OF THE
1970s CLEVELAND BROWNS

iUniverse books may be ordered through booksellers or by contacting:

iUniverse
1663 Liberty Drive
Bloomington, IN 47403
www.iuniverse.com
844-349-9409

Because of the dynamic nature of the Internet, any web addresses or links contained in this book may have changed since publication and may no longer be valid. The views expressed in this work are solely those of the author and do not necessarily reflect the views of the publisher, and the publisher hereby disclaims any responsibility for them.

Portions of this book were originally published in Bernie's Insiders/The Orange and Brown Report magazine.

Any people depicted in stock imagery provided by Getty Images are models, and such images are being used for illustrative purposes only. Certain stock imagery © Getty Images.

Cover photo – Greg Pruitt trying to elude Pittsburgh's Jack Lambert (58) and Mean Joe Greene, 1975 Malcolm W. Emmons/Wikimedia Commons

ISBN: 978-1-6632-6626-2 (sc)
ISBN: 978-1-6632-6627-9 (e)

Library of Congress Control Number: 2024917756

Print information available on the last page.

iUniverse rev. date: 08/27/2024

Contents

Preface

The title of this book, *The Forgotten Decade*, is so true when it comes to the history of the Cleveland Browns. The 1940s are remembered because the Browns dominated the All-America Football Conference to the tune of four championships in four years. The 1950s are remembered due to the team's seven NFL title-game appearances, three of which it won. The 1960s are recognized for the Browns' last league championship in 1964 plus three other title-game appearances. The 1980s are remembered because of the Kardiac Kids first and then the memorable five-year playoff run of the Bernie Kosar-led Browns, including three AFC Championship games. The team has not enjoyed much success since the 1990s, but that time period is recent enough that most Browns fans unfortunately can recall those mostly turbulent times.

What about the 1970s? The "disco decade" kind of gets lost in the shuffle – for several reasons. First, the Browns qualified for the postseason only twice, winning nary a game. They sunk to new lows in 1974 and 1975 with 4–10 and 3–11 records, respectively. They had a quarterback in Mike Phipps who failed to even come close to living up to expectations. They barely were above the .500 mark overall for the decade.

Despite the Browns' lack of success from 1970 to

1979, however, the team produced a number of intriguing tales. From Billy Andrews's memorable Monday night to Greg Pruitt in the Pittsburgh Steelers locker room to Thom Darden's foretelling to Howard Cosell, the Browns of the 1970s are proof positive that contending for championships is not the only factor in a team providing fascinating fables to its fans.

This book is not a chronological account of the 1970s Browns but rather a compilation of 23 stories in no particular order. It is meant to be a book in which readers can turn to any chapter of their liking at any time and enjoy it. Happy reading!

Acknowledgments

I would like to thank everyone at iUniverse in helping me put this book together. I would like to thank Ken Samelson for his outstanding editing. Thanks to my good friend and fellow author Rick Bowman for coming up with the book's title. Also, many thanks to the many people I interviewed.

1

THE BROWNS-BENGALS RIVALRY: A LEGEND'S REVENGE

It was a classic case of clashing egos—Paul Brown vs. Art Modell. From day one, when Modell purchased majority ownership of the Browns on March 21, 1961, it was a match made in hell. Unlike the previous owners, Modell wanted to be involved in the day-to-day operations of the club, including player personnel decisions. This didn't exactly endear him to Brown, who, as head coach and general manager, was accustomed to making player moves himself. As the Browns were sinking to mediocrity, an 8–5–1 record in 1961 and 7–6–1 in 1962, Modell's relationship with his head coach was rapidly deteriorating as well.

D-Day—Dismissal Day—came on January 9, 1963, when Modell shocked the city of Cleveland by announcing Browns's firing. A bitter, devastated Brown spent the following year in Cleveland free of grumbling players and interfering owners, then took up the quiet life at his home in La Jolla, California. Meanwhile, new head coach Blanton Collier, Brown's offensive backs coach, injected a much-needed drive into the stagnant franchise and led the team back to the upper echelon of the NFL. With Collier implementing a more wide-open offensive attack, the Browns won the NFL championship in his second year at the helm, 1964, and made three more title-game appearances in his tenure, which lasted through 1970.

With his former team busy playing in championship games, Browns decided to return to the game he loved. He and his family sold the city of Cincinnati on a professional football team, and the Brown family was awarded an American Football League (AFL) franchise on September 27, 1967, less than two months after Brown had been enshrined into the Pro Football Hall of Fame. Brown named his new team "Bengals" after two previous Cincinnati Bengals franchises that competed in two different AFLs in the late 1930s and early 1940s.

With his former team in mind, Brown outfitted the Bengals in attire similar to that of the Browns. Brown would be part-owner and general manager. He would also be head coach until retiring from the sidelines after the 1975 season. After two seasons in the AFL, the Bengals joined the NFL in 1970 and were placed in the AFC Central Division with Pittsburgh, Houston, and, yes, Cleveland.

Not coincidentally, the Browns and Bengals were matched up for an exhibition game on August 29, 1970, at brand new Riverfront Stadium in Cincinnati. The Bengals were sky high, wanting to give their coach a victory in his first meeting with his old team in front of

57,112 fans, the largest crowd ever to see a sporting event in the Queen City up to that point. The Browns burst the Bengals' bubble, at least in the opening quarter. A 41-yard pass from quarterback Bill Nelsen to tight end Milt Morin and a one-yard run by running back Leroy Kelly gave the visitors a 14–0 lead. The Bengals, however, got on track in the second quarter. A pair of one-yard runs by Jess Phillips and a 43-yard field goal by Horst Muhlmann gave them a 17–14 halftime lead.

Don Cockroft's 39-yard trey tied the score in the third quarter. Soon after, Bengals defensive end Royce Berry put the home team back on top as he was in the right place at the right time. Nelsen was hit and the ball darted right into the arms of Berry, who returned the interception 40 yards for a touchdown. The Bengals put the game away in the fourth quarter when quarterback and future Bengals head coach Sam Wyche passed six yards to Chip Myers to make the score 31–17. The Bengals went on to win, 31–24.

Cincinnati's victory may have been just a preseason game, but Paul Brown finally got the revenge he longed for.

The two teams' much-anticipated first regular-season meeting came in week four on October 11 at Cleveland in front of a throng of 83,520 fans. The Bengals started fast, taking a 10–2 lead after one quarter. It was 17-16 Bengals at the half. A pair of short touchdown passes from Nelsen to Kelly and Morin had kept the Browns in the game. Down 20–16 entering the fourth quarter, the Browns took the lead and kept it on the strength of one-yard touchdown runs by Kelly and running back Bo Scott, winning, 30–27. Thus, round one in the games that counted went to Art Modell. Brown refused to shake Collier's hand after the game. Five weeks later, on November 15, the Bengals won the rematch in Riverfront, 14–10.

"That was Art Modell's most intense rivalry. Both he and Paul Brown put up a front that their friendship was still intact. It was not," said Dan Coughlin, a former longtime sportswriter for *The Plain Dealer* who covered the Browns part time in the 1970s. "Blanton's daughter Kay spent some time with me in our house in Lakewood. She revealed to me how Paul Brown broke Blanton's heart when he turned his back on him. When Blanton accepted the job as his successor, Blanton said, 'I called Paul and told him I would not take this job without his blessing.' Well, how can you tell him, 'No, I want you to turn down the job?' So Paul Brown said, 'Of course,' but he didn't mean it. He resented Blanton intensely for taking the job. The one thing that was unusual was the intensity of Brown's resentment. Kay remembered as a little kid growing up how close the families were. They would go on vacations together, Paul Brown and Blanton and their children! Kay remembered sitting on Paul Brown's lap at Blanton's home in Kentucky in the offseason. The two families would get together frequently in the offseason. All of that stopped when Paul was fired and Blanton took over. Their friendship ended. Kay remembered how Paul Brown was so kind to her. She would be practicing playing the piano, and he would try to play a few notes along with her. That's how close they were. But then Paul Brown went stone cold on Blanton and his family. It's a shame. The intensity of that rivalry was fueled by Paul Brown. Blanton couldn't really take it as just another game either."

Said Billy Andrews, a Browns linebacker from 1967 to 1974, "When Paul Brown did not shake in my opinion Hall of Fame coach Blanton Collier's hand after that first game, that put fire in my veins."

"That was weird, that was tense … you know, the old coach coming back. It was rough. It was a very, very, very emotional game, no question about it," said Steve King, the Browns' historian for ClevelandBrowns.com from 2004 to 2013 and the editor of BrownsDailyDose. com since 2015. "Blanton Collier went across the field to see Brown, and Brown just kind of waved him off and ignored him and ran to the locker room. It hurt Collier because he genuinely respected their friendship. They may have shaken hands before the game, but after the game Paul Brown wanted no part of Collier. The coaches always meet at the middle of the field after a game. Brown felt like he had been blindsided and blackmailed by his friend."

By the time the Bengals knocked the Browns out of playoff contention with a 16–12 win on December 16, 1979, the two teams' last game of the 1970s, each team had won 10 games in the series. The Brown-Modell feud remained as hot as ever. The Browns-Bengals rivalry? It was red hot the first couple years but, to many people, it did not compare to the Browns-Steelers rivalry once Pittsburgh got its act together in 1972.

"I think the first couple years, the Browns-Bengals rivalry exceeded the Browns-Steelers rivalry," said Mike Peticca, who covered the Browns part time for the Associated Press in the late 1970s and was a Browns fan living in Akron in the first part of the decade. "The Browns-Bengals rivalry probably got as much media coverage as possible in those days. I remember leading into those games, they were maybe hyped as much as playoff games. It kind of wore off a little after that, though. The Steelers-Browns rivalry eventually passed the Browns-Bengals rivalry, started by the 1972 Steelers at Browns game] won by the Browns on Don Cockroft's field goal with eight seconds remaining]."

"Browns-Steelers was a great geographical rivalry, it was a rough-and-tumble rivalry, but it wasn't much of a rivalry because the Steelers just had not been very good," said King. "So coming into the '70s, really the rivalry I think was more so with Cincinnati because of Paul Brown."

"The rivalry with the Bengals was nothing compared to the Steelers rivalry," said Thom Darden, a Browns free safety from 1972 to 1974 and 1976 to 1981.

"The Bengals rivalry didn't compare to the one with the Steelers," said Doug Dieken, who played offensive left tackle for Cleveland from 1971 to 1984.

"I don't think the Bengals rivalry compared to the Steelers rivalry, but there was some bad blood because of Blanton taking over for Paul Brown," said Jerry Sherk, who played mainly right defensive tackle for the Browns from 1970 to 1981. "As a rookie, it was hard for me to, all at once, get fired up and go, 'Those guys are really the bad guys and we're the good guys.' But over the years, since it was an intrastate rivalry, it had something extra, but not because Paul Brown was the creator of the Bengals or the head coach but because it was kind of like fighting over Ohio turf."

Modell and the Rooneys, the Steelers owners, were friends, but Modell and Paul Brown were on opposite ends. It was very personal. That was the big rivalry for Modell, and that was the big rivalry throughout the organization. The Browns wanted to win that game.

"By the end of the '70s, though," said King, "the Steelers rivalry was bigger because it had grown. To get to the division championship you had to go through Pittsburgh, and that was the focus as the decade went on, but for Modell it was still personal with Paul Brown. There's the story about [head coach] Sam Rutigliano getting on the bus on December 21, 1980, for the season-ending game the Browns needed to win to win the AFC Central title, and Modell patting him on the back and saying, 'Hey, if we don't win today, hey, it's been a great season,' and Sam said, 'Bullshit. You know as well as I do you want to win this game. The guy up in the suites today will be the guy you fired, Paul Brown.' So Modell's feeling about Brown was still personal, and Sam understood it."

There were those, however, who felt the rivalry with the Bengals was just as bitter as the rivalry with the Steelers throughout the 1970s.

"When the Browns and Bengals played for the first time in 1970, only seven years had passed since Art Modell had fired Paul Brown," said Michael Cuomo, a Browns fan who grew up in Rochester, New York, and whose connection to the Browns was his older brother and father becoming fans in the late 1950s and early 1960s, passing that fandom on to him. Browns games were on television a lot in Rochester in the 1960s. He lived in Steubenville in the late 1970s. "My father loved Paul Brown, so he had a soft spot for Paul Brown and the Bengals. He wanted the Browns to win, but he had all the respect in the world for Paul Brown. I didn't share that opinion because, to me, it was like, 'Oh, Paul Brown was here so long ago.'"

"Browns-Bengals was a huge rivalry," Andrews said. "It was every bit as intense as the Steelers rivalry."

Art Modell
Jerry Sherk/Wikimedia Commons

2

JERRY SHERK'S NEAR-DEATH EXPERIENCE

Imagine waking up in the middle of the night, only to see a stranger standing at the foot of your bed, repeating over and over, "God has put a terrible burden on you."

Jerry Sherk did not have to imagine. It happened to him. It was two weeks before Thanksgiving 1979, and the Browns' right defensive tackle was a patient at the Cleveland Clinic. "It was a doctor, an older guy, making night rounds," Sherk, drugged heavily on morphine at the time, recalled. "I was in a dream-like state, but I remember thinking, 'What does this guy know about my situation that I don't know?' It kind of freaked me out."

Sherk had a right to be concerned. After all, his left knee was the size of an NFL football. Disaster had struck not long before when, on November 4, he was stricken with a serious staph infection in a game against the Philadelphia Eagles at Veterans Stadium. "I had a boil on my arm and scraped it on the turf," remembered Sherk.

No big deal, he figured – that is, until the next day during a film session at practice when he felt shooting pain in his left knee. "It went away for a while," Sherk recalled, "but that evening when I drove home, the pain returned and it was unbearable. By the time I got home, I had to crawl from my car to my house as I couldn't put any weight on the knee. Bill Tessendorf was our assistant trainer, and he lived nearby, so I called him. He came right over and drove me to the [Cleveland] Clinic. Every pothole in the road that Bill's car hit made me yell in pain. The pain was 12 on a scale of one to 10."

Doctors cultured fluid from the center of Sherk's knee, which had been operated on once before. A few days later, they concluded that to his knee is exactly where the staph infection spread. Done for the season, Sherk not only missed out on the stretch run of the first edition of the Kardiac Kids, he was in very serious condition. Surgery by Browns team physician John Bergfeld was next. "They opened the knee," Sherk said, "and it wasn't pretty. I was told by a surgical assistant years later that when they took a scalpel to my knee, [the knee] fairly exploded across the room."

Once the procedure was completed, doctors filled two holes they had cut above Sherk's knee with saline solution drips. Meanwhile, a pump on two holes in the bottom of his knee sucked fluids out. A week or two later, Sherk's high fever led doctors to believe the infection was still lurking and that the great defensive tackle's life was actually in danger. Amputation was an option. "I had teams of doctors coming in three or four times a day,"

Sherk remembered, "just like on the TV shows, so I knew something was up."

Doctors later realized the fever was merely the result of an antibiotic to which Sherk had a reaction. Sherk, who shed 40 pounds in his nearly one-month stay at the Clinic, began a strenuous rehab period, then took a stab at salvaging his career. He started the 1980 season opener at New England. It would be his last start. "My knee was so weak," he said. "I was ineffective and knew that I was done for the year."

Thus, Sherk missed out on part two of the Kardiac Kids. He took one last crack at a comeback in 1981 as a third-down pass rusher. "My knee was stronger but still weak," he said. "I knew it was time to quit when I recounted my season—zero sacks for a pass-rush specialist is not a good thing."

Sherk decided to call it a career. "I quit football," he said, "before football decided to quit me."

Sherk, fortunate in that he endures very little pain today—"I owe it to Dr. Bergfeld that I still have a leg and a life," he said—would have been a sure Hall of Famer, some say, had he stayed healthy for a few more years.

A second-round draft choice of the Browns in 1970 out of Oklahoma State University where he played right defensive end, Sherk was one of the greatest defensive players not only in Browns history but in the entire history of the NFL.

Just how great was he?

Well, in 1976 Sherk was named the NFL Defensive Player of the Year by the Newspaper Enterprise Association, beating out the likes of Jack Lambert, Mean Joe Greene, Randy White, and Alan Page. Future Hall of Famers. Members of some of the fiercest defenses of all time— Pittsburgh's "Steel Curtain," Dallas's "Doomsday," and Minnesota's "Purple People Eaters." That's right! A member of the 1976 Cleveland Browns, a team whose 9–5 record was the franchise's first winning season in three years, was honored as the best defensive player in the NFL over guys on teams that were perennial Super Bowl contenders. Sherk's Pro Bowl appearance that year was his fourth straight. He was named to various All-AFC defensive teams in 1975 and 1976.

Besides shining on the football field at Oklahoma State, the athletically gifted Sherk used his natural strength to excel on the wrestling mat where, as a heavyweight, he won the Big Eight title and advanced to nationals as a junior. He credits his experience as a big-time college mat man in aiding him on the gridiron.

"I had developed a good workout ethic because wrestlers are maniacs," he said. "I used balance and conditioning more than others. The Browns didn't have much of a weight room when I got there, so I did a lot of push-ups and sit-ups and running.

"Being a wrestler also helped me with the mental part of the game. I imagined during games that it was just me and that guy across from me—and this really helped.

Also, for some reason, I really 'wanted it.' I wanted to do well and hear the cheers."

Sherk had a good mind—an analytic one—for the game of football with or without wrestling. "I could see what it took to be successful," he said. "Very often, the formula was simple: Get in better shape than anyone and be aggressive on each and every play, even if we were losing 30–0, which we often were."

Dick Modzelewski, Cleveland's defensive line coach/defensive coordinator for much of the 1970s, held Sherk in the highest regard. "Jerry's a student of the game, he always studied it. Everybody looked up to him," he said. "He not only was the best tackle I ever coached, he was also the smartest."

So smart, in fact, that the mentor actually learned a thing or two from the student regarding the tackle position. "Jerry taught me about extending the arms and coming off the ball with full extension.," Modzelewski, a one-time Browns defensive tackle himself, said. "He had separation between him and the offensive player. Today's linemen come off the ball standing straight up, chest-to-chest, instead of full extension. Jerry was slow in the 40-yard dash, but all I cared about was how fast he was within 10 yards. He was quick from his position to the quarterback. He hustled all the time, in practice too. He'd pursue players and chase them down."

Sherk credits Modzelewski for making him the player he was. "Dick was a former player, so he knew what it took," he said. "He knew exactly how to handle me. He would leave me in games as a rookie, even when it was hurting the team somewhat. He would tell me, 'I'm leaving you in so your confidence won't be broken, and this will even help the team in the long run.' There are few coaches with that kind of intuition and feel for the game and the players they are coaching.

"He would also shield us from what the other coaches would say about our techniques—if they felt we should change them—even if it was the head coach. It's rare for a coach to do that.

"I will always be indebted to Mo."

Upon arriving at Hiram College for training camp in 1970, Sherk and the other rookies were fortunate that they were spared the annual hazing, for the veteran players were on strike at the time. However, Sherk did get "picked on" in his very first regular-season game— not only by the New York Jets, who ran the ball in his direction all game long, but also by Howard Cosell of all people. Cosell was in Cleveland Municipal Stadium that evening as part of ABC's broadcast crew for the first ever *Monday Night Football* telecast.

"Cosell always chose one thing to talk about throughout the entire broadcast, no matter the sport," said Sherk, who later viewed the game on tape delay. "Well, he chose me that night. He kept saying, 'The Jets are going to pick on that rookie Sherk.' And they did. Cosell kept kind of hammering on me."

But even when Sherk, who went up against veteran guard Randy Rasmussen that evening, came up with a fine play, the rookie still couldn't shake the announcers' hazing—even if it *was* a mistake. "I batted down a pass from Joe Namath," he laughed, "and the announcer—not sure which one—said, 'What a play by [teammate] Jack Gregory!'"

"Randy Rasmussen, one of the best offensive linemen in the game at the time," Steve King said, "really had his way with Sherk that night, really kind of dominated him."

Sherk defended himself against what Cosell did in that first Monday night game: "What I came to realize—I saw Cosell call a number of games after that plus boxing matches and so forth —was that he was a great personality with a great vocabulary and a great, dramatic delivery, but he was not a great analyst, he was not even a good analyst. In fact, I can remember sitting with Brian Sipe one time, and we were watching Cosell call a boxing match. Brian turned to me and said, 'Is he watching the same match that we're watching?' Cosell would get a predetermined idea, and he would go with it."

It took a few years for Sherk, like most players, to adapt to the NFL and hit his prime. "I took lots of bumps at first," he said. "You feel like you're a target when you're young and inexperienced. Helmets kept hitting me full force in those early days. Later, *I* became the missile, putting my helmet on running backs almost at will."

Sherk was a member of some quality Browns teams at the start of his career, including the 1972 club that came within a whisker of stunning the undefeated Miami Dolphins in a Christmas Eve playoff in the Orange Bowl.

"I was fired up for that game," Sherk recalled. "I remember I was so excited that I didn't settle down until the second quarter. I told myself at the time that there's getting too up for a game and that I wouldn't let that happen again."

Ironically, as Sherk was hitting his prime, the Browns were sinking to their worst period in history. Sherk was one of the few bright spots on some pretty average and awful—4–10 in 1974, 3–11 in 1975—teams. He blames the club's lack of "keeping up with the Joneses" for the downfall.

"From my perspective," he said, "they didn't 'modernize' and keep up with the AFC—old AFL—teams. Scouting had advanced, and the Browns limped along with a handful of pro scouts instead of expanding the scouting department and getting more or less scientific."

One of the highlights of Sherk's Defensive Lineman of the Year season of 1976 occurred in the season opener against the Jets in Cleveland. "There's a picture in one of the Browns media guides of that game," said Steve King, "in which Rasmussen is lying on the ground, and Sherk's just bent over right over top of him. That encapsulates the growth of Jerry Sherk from that first game as a rookie in 1970 to 1976. As much as he got dominated by Rasmussen in the 1970 game, he dominated Rasmussen in the 1976 game."

The season before, Sherk won the NFL's first Mack Truck Bulldog Award, which was an award back then that was voted on by the offensive linemen in the league of which defensive player they thought was the toughest to block.

Things began to turn around for the team later in the decade. Sherk, although slowed somewhat by age, was still going strong and enjoying a tremendous 1979 season when the staph infection disaster occurred.

Many people feel Sherk should be in the Pro Football Hall of Fame.

"To me, he was clearly the best defensive lineman of the '70s for the Browns. I think he should be in the Hall of Fame, I really do. He played a long time," King said. "For a decade, he was a great player in a division that had a lot of great defensive players. He wasn't just a great player and tough and physical, but he was smart. He'd sit there and turn sideways, put his ear directly to the line of scrimmage when the other team was huddling and try to catch a word or a phrase or a number to get an idea of what the play might be. He studied the offensive linemen he was facing. He was very, very, very quick. He'd shoot a gap and he'd be across the line of scrimmage. He was an almost unblockable player."

"I think, if it was baseball, where the criteria is

becoming less strict it seems, Sherk would be in the Hall of Fame," said Mike Peticca. "In reality, maybe he needed a couple more healthy years. It's a shame he got hurt. He belongs in the Hall of Fame. By 1972 at the latest, he was one of the very best, and he maintained that status right until the staph infection in '79. He probably had an edge over virtually any lineman he faced as far as quickness, agility, technique, intelligence, and strength. All of the things that make a guy good, he was among the elite. How many defensive linemen are actually fun to watch? He was fun to isolate your eyes on and watch! Just from a fan's standpoint, I don't know how many guys you do that with."

"I think he should be in the Hall of Fame," Doug Dieken said. "I think, had he not got the staph infection, he'd *be* in the Hall of Fame. He was unbelievable. He wasn't the fastest guy but, because he'd been a wrestler, he just knew moves and how to do the hands and use the leverage and everything."

The accolades just keep coming.

"Jerry Sherk is probably my favorite player of all time. He was the best defensive tackle I ever saw," said Mike McLain, who covered the Browns for the *Warren Tribune-Chronicle* for many years after the 1970s but is still knowledgeable on the 1970s Browns and who was raised in Warren. "He was the only defensive player the Browns had then who could've started for the Steelers defense back then. You put Jerry Sherk at tackle on those

Steelers teams, he would've made one of the best defenses ever even better."

"Jerry played hard every play," said Fred Hoaglin, a Browns center from 1966 to 1972. "He was a tremendous competitor, and he played to win every play."

Once his playing days were done, Sherk ventured into photography, real estate development, and school counseling before settling into his current occupation in the mid-1990s (now on a part-time basis) as a consultant for mentoring programs. A pioneer in the field who works from his home in Encinitas, California, Sherk, who owns a master's degree in counseling psychology, is the founder of Mentor Management Systems (MMS).

"I originally studied psychology to deal with my own transition out of football," said Sherk, "but I soon realized that the subject of 'life transitions' isn't only for ex-NFL ballplayers—everyone deals with chaotic and changing events—and I guess that's how I got into the mentoring business. I found mentoring to be a good way to help children through adolescence and older people with job and life changes.

"At MMS we assist all kinds of organizations in creating or improving mentoring programs."

Although Sherk's main focus through the years has been youth mentoring, he and his group also help a variety of adult mentoring programs such as government employees and social workers. Sherk assisted the US Department of Labor in two nationwide programs that mentor recently released prisoners. He ran a group mentoring program in the city school system in San Diego. He writes training materials for Los Angeles Team Mentoring, a program that serves 1,200 youths annually in the most impoverished areas of that metropolis and also works with a group called the California Mentoring Partnership, an advocacy group. He develops mentoring webinars, too.

Sherk realizes that his current profession has brought him full circle.

"It's funny," he says. "As I introduce myself during the many trainings I do, I often say, 'I used to be a mean guy—I tore people apart [in the NFL].' But now I'm spending the second part of my life putting people together—in mentoring relationships."

Sherk spends countless hours on his laptop computer—but not necessarily behind his desk at home.

"I'm a wireless guy," he said. "I sit in coffee shops and write—sometimes for half a day at a time—and then bike to the next coffee shop with my computer in my backpack in order to take a break and get exercise. I'm sure people are wondering who the old guy is with the backpack. My secret desire is to write the great American novel about my experiences in the NFL."

Although 76 years old, the 6-foot-5 Sherk does not look anywhere near his age. In fact, his weight of 240 pounds is exactly the same as it was during his playing days. "I bike a lot while listening to Fleetwood Mac and a little Rod Stewart—and look out at the surfers catching waves. I have a folding bike that folds up to about 24 inches by 24 inches, and I throw it in the back of my car and then unfold it and keep going. I do a lot of walking, too."

Sherk, who also enjoys reading and traveling, has been married to the former Annie Kelley of Lakewood for 41 years. The couple has two grown children, Mike, a historical and genealogical researcher and librarian, and Hannah, a staff writer for a magazine.

When Sherk was asked about his greatest memory from his days in the orange and brown, his answer did not include a particular game or play. Fittingly—considering walking is a passion of his today—it was the pregame stroll down the Cleveland Stadium tunnel from the locker room to the dugout.

"It was very dim," he recalled, "maybe one General Electric light every 20 to 30 feet. You could hear the crowd start roaring and see the light at the end of the tunnel. Very emotional."

Emotional is also an apt way to describe Sherk's feelings about the Browns' move to Baltimore and the subsequent bulldozing of the Stadium. He felt so strongly about the old ballpark that, soon before it was demolished in 1996, he and former teammate—and close friend—Brian Sipe actually hosted an hour-long television program titled *The Brown Blues* in which the two took an emotion-filled journey through just about every nook and cranny of the structure, including a saunter on the roof!

"We wanted to have closure on our Browns experience, especially if the Browns were not going to exist anymore," said Sherk, who also enjoyed a game of catch with Sipe, the ex-Kardiac kingpin. The former teammates' personal farewell to the Stadium was part of a two-week-long visit to the North Coast in which they mingled with, and interviewed for the TV show, several other former Browns.

"It was a wonderful couple of weeks," said Sherk, who still roots for the Browns to this day even from 2,500 miles away. "We learned a great deal about Browns history. I gained great respect for players who were in an older generation—Bill Willis, Marion Motley, Dante Lavelli, and so forth."

Michael Cuomo's memory of attending a Browns-Vikings game in 1975 perfectly encapsulates just how great of a player Sherk was.

"We got beat bad," he said. "I was sitting in the end zone watching the game, and I'm saying to myself, *This Jerry Sherk's making every tackle all over the place.* The next day in the *Plain Dealer* [Vikings head coach] Bud Grant answered the question 'Is there anything you didn't do well?' And he says, 'Well, we didn't block Jerry Sherk. He was phenomenal.'"

Jerry Sherk, 1972
Jerry Sherk/Wikimedia Commons

3

THE MISTAKE BY THE LAKE

Cleveland Municipal Stadium (in 1978 the name changed to Cleveland Stadium) meant a lot to a lot of different people, from players to fans to media members. One thing, however, that was certain for the big edifice by Lake Erie was that it brought joy, even in its later, decrepit years, to many people, especially Browns players.

"I'd been there as a kid, so I knew a little bit about the stadium when I was drafted by the Browns," Thom Darden said. "Running out on that field from the tunnel, that was always an exciting experience. Seeing 80,000 … even when we weren't that good, we had 80,000 people in there. Especially coming into the baseball infield and down into the bleachers area was always interesting. Going from one end zone to the lake, that was a beautiful site, but you forget about all of that stuff when play started. The field was always in pretty decent shape. The baseball infield made it kind of difficult because you would run into dirt and sand, and it was hard to keep your footing sometimes. I loved standing down there watching the people fighting up in the stands. It always happened when we played the Steelers."

"When that stadium was full— particularly the night games we played against the Steelers once a year—it was loud," said Gary Collins, a Browns wide receiver from 1962 to 1971. "My last game at the Stadium we played the Baltimore Colts in a playoff game, and I dropped a couple passes, it was bad weather. That's the most passes I ever dropped in my career, and I heard it. I got booed."

Said Billy Andrews, "It was a life experience to play before 80,000 people almost every game but in particular the first Monday night game. My whole career in that stadium was unbelievable to me. I'm an old country boy, so that kind of experience just never leaves you."

"It was a great place to play," Fred Hoaglin said. "The fans loved us; they made a lot of noise. The noise didn't bother us on the field, though, because it was such a big stadium. We were still able to hear the play called in the huddle and the quarterback calling the signals. It was just always fun to go in there. Because I played center, I got to be the first guy introduced, the first guy to run out on the field, when we played at home."

"There were times when the crowd was so into it and so loud," added Jerry Sherk. "The sound was so all encompassing and all pervasive that sometimes the roar was continuous through the whole game. It felt like the sound was vibrating from the grass up into my body."

"The first part of the season," Doug Dieken said, "because it was a dual-purpose stadium, had the baseball infield, so you'd go from grass to this hard dirt, so it wasn't the best of situations. And then, if you went to the other end, the goalpost was almost on top of what they now call The Dawg Pound. If you were a wide receiver on that end and you were running a slant route you could run out of room real quick."

Michael Cuomo went to one or two Browns home games per season and said he remembers the steel pillars that were in the way while he was trying to watch the game.

"When you didn't have season tickets in that stadium," he said, "chances were you were going to buy an individual game ticket that was in the bleachers. On those occasions where we weren't in the end zone, it was worth it to have to lean one way or the other just to watch the game because just being there was so much fun. And if you got the better seats that were in front of the poles, you could really see the plays develop. The thing that really stood out to me was the roar of the crowd that was unmatched. I don't know what it was. I don't know if it was the roof that held the noise in or what, but we had that roof, and it was a great protection against the rain if you were sitting in the upper deck. Also, I didn't come from a big drinking family. I would go there to watch the games, and I was really surprised at how some people got so totally drunk at the games."

"If the fans complained about the stadium, they never showed it by boycotting the stadium. Nobody stayed away because of the stadium," Dan Coughlin said.

"People took the steel beams as a part of life, that that's what happens when you built a stadium in 1930. People put up with it. I loved the old Stadium."

Covering Browns games in the 1970s was quite an experience.

"The football press box was at the very top of the upper deck," remembered Coughlin. "It was the worst press box in the NFL. We were crammed in shoulder to shoulder in there."

"They had these old elevators that would bring you from ground level all the way up to the press box," Mike Peticca said. "Even though the press box was way at the top of the Stadium, it was great from sight considerations. It was an ideal place to see the game. It was easy to pick up the uniform numbers. That press box probably ranged from one 40 yard line to the other. Above the press box on the roof was where the announcers were, so that gives some insight that it was great from a sight standpoint even though it was far away."

The plumbing system in the press box was pretty primitive, according to Peticca.

"There was one little so-called restroom in the press box, and that press box was always packed with around 60 people," he said. "Of course, both guys and girls had to use it. It had one toilet and one urinal. There was a cheap rug that ran throughout the press box, and by sometime in the first half that rug would get soaked with urine."

Peticca and his cohorts who had to go into the locker

rooms after games would leave the press box usually early to mid-fourth quarter in order to make sure they got their quotes for their articles.

"We'd always take the elevator down, and we'd watch the rest of the game on the sidelines by the Browns bench because that was the only way to logistically to get to the locker rooms in time."

"It was always cool to walk through the baseball dugout and the tunnel that led up to the locker room," Mike McLain said. "I always thought it was a privilege because it was like being in a submarine, following all these big guys walking up and down that tunnel."

Steve King understands why old Cleveland Stadium has been criticized, but he feels it gets a bad rap.

"When you were in there and you walked those portals, you knew that you were walking in the steps of great men that walked there," he said. "And not just football, baseball as well. Feller, DiMaggio, Graham, and Groza and Jim Brown and on and on and on. You just felt special. To me, that place was always an honor and a privilege. I never looked at it as, 'Well, this didn't work' or 'That didn't work.' I went to Fenway Park to see an Indians-Red Sox game in 1995. It was cramped, but it was special. It was Fenway Park. Those old ballparks were great. I understand all the accommodations for today's fans and whatever, and I'm all for that. But don't badmouth Cleveland Stadium. It was really special. A lot of great things happened there."

4

THOM DARDEN: KARDIAC PROMISE

Guarantees gone bad. They happen from time to time in the world of professional sports.

Prophecies by pro athletes make for good bulletin board material, and that's about it. Most of the time, the foretelling does not go as planned, making the athlete look like a fool. But on the rare occasion when an athlete backs up his promise, when he "walks the walk" after "talking the talk," he looks like nothing short of a genius.

Perhaps the most famous athlete guarantee that came true was Babe Ruth's legendary "called shot" during Game Three of the 1932 World Series when the Yankees slugger pointed toward the center field bleachers in Wrigley Field, allegedly gesturing that he would hit a home run—and then did. Joe Namath's memorable pledge of victory three days before his New York Jets upset the Baltimore Colts in Super Bowl III is up there, too.

What many Browns fans probably are unaware of is that Cleveland, too—like New York and other sports towns across the country—owns a piece of the "guarantee gone good" pie.

Thanks to former Browns safety Thom Darden.

The date was September 23, 1979. Darden, in his seventh season with the Browns, was hosting his weekly radio show, "All-Pro Jazz," on "The Buzzard"— 100.7-FM/WMMS. The next evening, Darden and the Browns—recently dubbed the "Kardiac Kids"—would take an unblemished 3-0 record into a *Monday Night Football* clash with the also unbeaten Dallas Cowboys— America's Team—at mammoth Cleveland Stadium.

Darden's guest on the radio show that night before the game was none other than Howard Cosell, who along with Frank Gifford and "Dandy" Don Meredith, would call the game for ABC. Darden made a prediction to the living legend on air.

"I told him, 'Howard, I'm gonna intercept a pass tomorrow.'"

That was quite a bold statement from Darden. After all, Dallas quarterback Roger Staubach had not thrown a pick in his last 150 passes dating back to the previous season. But the next evening, with the Browns already leading, 13–0, early on and the Cowboys at their own 35 yard line in front of more than 80,000 howling fans, Roger "The Dodger," in his usual shotgun formation, fired a pass over the middle intended for Ron Springs. Darden, the free safety, stepped in front of the Cowboys running back, caught the ball, and took his foretelling one step further by returning it 39 yards for a touchdown that not only gave the underdog Browns a 20–0 lead before the visitors had gained even a single first down, but also brought the huge stadium to a deafening din.

"That was certainly one of my greater moments," said Darden. "That place was rockin'. The electricity in that stadium that night was unbelievable."

Darden admitted there was much more to that interception than met the eye. "I can't take credit for that play," he said. "In the film study during the week, we saw that Staubach would have a formation where he had three guys on one side, to the defense's right side generally. And the inside two would come downfield at that time and set a screen, and then the outside guy would run underneath. Staubach would hit him because he was wide open all the time. So when we saw that formation, I was supposed to fake like I was going to the deep middle and then come up. Staubach was throwing the ball to the inside guy coming across the field, and I stepped right in front of him and got the ball, and obviously there was no one there, so I waltzed into the end zone. I give 100 percent credit to our secondary coach for that play."

To top things off, after the pick six, Cosell informed the nation about Darden's prophecy the previous evening. The Browns went on to win, 26–7.

Another reason Darden's memorable interception was unforgettable to him?

"I grew up a Browns fan!" he said.

Born in nearby Sandusky, Darden began playing football in the sixth grade as a running back and quarterback. After playing quarterback again in the seventh grade, he was switched to wide receiver and defensive back the next year. This was about the time Darden realized that he preferred the defensive side of the ball.

"I didn't like getting hit," he admitted. "It hurt."

Instead, Darden would go on to inflict pain on many a receiver during the next two decades.

Darden was a good player as a young boy, but nothing special.

"Everybody thought I was too skinny, too small, and too slow," he said. "They figured I could play in high school but that I'd never make it in college."

Sandusky High School, at the time, was considered one of the finest programs in the state of Ohio. Darden started at receiver, cornerback, and safety on the freshman team. It was at this time that Darden, with the guidance of an assistant coach, began studying film, not a regular practice for high school rookies.

"He taught us how to study film and what to look for not only in our own play but in others," Darden recalled.

Perhaps it helped.

"I don't think we lost a game," Darden said of his freshman squad.

Darden, who finally started to pack on some pounds due to weightlifting, played receiver and defensive back on the undefeated junior varsity team as a sophomore in 1965, and did see some mop-up duty at cornerback and safety that year on the also unbeaten varsity team that won the mythical Class AAA state championship in both the Associated Press and United Press International (UPI) polls. As a junior Darden started at receiver, cornerback, and safety on the varsity squad that went undefeated again but did not repeat as state champion.

Due to an injury to the team captain, Darden, all of 173 pounds, was switched to—believe it or not—middle linebacker for his senior year in addition to his receiving duties. Darden, whose team lost one game that year, said it was the best thing that ever happened to him.

"It toughened me up," he said.

Although Sandusky sits almost smack in the middle between Columbus and Ann Arbor, Michigan, Darden rooted for neither Ohio State or Michigan.

"I didn't like Ohio State," he said, "because they were three yards and a cloud of dust, and being a wide receiver, I liked the teams who threw the ball. I didn't have an affinity to Michigan either."

That is, until he visited Ann Arbor his senior year.

"I fell in love with the campus," he said. "I also liked Bump Elliott, the coach."

Recruited by several schools, Darden accepted a full ride to "That School Up North." With the NCAA rule prohibiting freshmen from playing varsity ball still in effect, Darden played receiver and defensive back on the Wolverines' freshmen team in 1968. By the time his sophomore year—Bo Schembechler's first as head coach—rolled around, Darden was strictly playing defensive back. He believes the decision was made during a scrimmage in spring ball his freshman year.

"I think I was running second team," he said, "and I had a couple of good hits against the varsity. Right then, Bo told me that was where he was going to play me."

Darden, the free safety, was one of only a handful of sophomores to start for the 1969 Wolverines. He and his teammates took a 7–2 record into the Ohio State game in Ann Arbor on November 22. The defending national champion Buckeyes were 8–0, ranked number one in the nation in both polls, and brought a 22-game winning streak into Michigan Stadium.

"They'd just been obliterating everybody they played," Darden remembered. "I'll never forget, they came into the stadium in pregame and came down and took three quarters of the field for their warmups. Bo was highly upset. So we come in the locker room after warmups, he was … fit to be tied. He was saying, 'We can't allow these guys to come into our stadium and take over three quarters of our field for warmups!' At the end of his speech, he smashed his fist through the blackboard! It was like, 'Oh-h-h my goodness!' That whole locker room erupted and guys were so fired up, I never experienced anything like that ever again.

"We get down on the field and just seemed like we had control of that game the entire way."

Michigan shocked the world by upsetting Ohio State, 24–12, to win the Big Ten title.

"It was unbelievable," Darden said, "definitely my most memorable team moment at Michigan. Our celebration lasted about a week."

Darden and his teammates lost to the University of Southern California, 10–3, in the Rose Bowl with Schembechler in the hospital due to a heart attack the night before.

"We learned about it when we got in the locker room before the game," Darden said. "It was like a thousand-pound weight fell on the team. There was no enthusiasm, people were lethargic … it just was not the same team. It didn't seem like our heart was in it, not to make that an excuse. It wasn't the greatest USC team, but they were a pretty good team."

Darden switched to cornerback his junior year in 1970, and had five interceptions (tying for the team lead) to help Michigan to a 9–1 record, but the Wolverines fell, 20–9, to conference champ Ohio State in the revenge match in Columbus. In Darden's senior year Michigan finished 11–1 and, with the conference title already clinched, beat a so-so Buckeyes team, 10–7, in Ann Arbor. Darden, back at free safety, had a team-leading four picks that year (for 163 return yards), including one against Ohio State that will forever live in his memory.

"They were driving for the go-ahead touchdown," he said. "I didn't think I was going to intercept the ball.

All I was trying to do was make sure the receiver didn't catch it. And the next thing I knew, it was in my hands!"

Michigan's national championship hopes went up in flames in a 13–11 loss to underdog Stanford in the Rose Bowl.

"We shut them down pretty well on defense," Darden said, "but we couldn't complete a pass or run the ball. We didn't do anything on offense.

"We lost two Rose Bowls in my career, and we gave both of them away."

Darden, who was first-team All-Big Ten his last two years and an All-American his senior year, did not particularly like Schembechler at first.

"He was forceful, loud, he was always yelling, and he challenged you all the time," he said. "You never could do enough to satisfy him. He pushed you to be the best that you could possibly be. There was never a time that he didn't push you. I really didn't appreciate him, though, until I got into the pros. I realized that his constant pushing is what made me a better player."

Darden was chosen by the Browns with the 18th overall pick of the 1972 NFL draft. After taking part in the "All-American banquet tour," as Darden called it, and playing in the Hula Bowl and the College All-Star Game against the defending Super Bowl champion Cowboys—"Bob Hayes ran by me so fast one time, it was like I was standing still," Darden recalled—the rookie reported to training camp at Hiram College.

The 6-foot-2, 195-pound Darden more than lived up to his first-round billing, starting every game at strong safety as a rookie, and doing it well. He got off to a rough start, though.

"I got beat on a play the first game of the season against the Packers. I got outsmarted," he said. "They had this play where their tight end acted like he was blocking down. My read was when the right end blocks down, that means there's going to be a run, so you come up. Well, the tight end acted like he was blocking down, I came up, and he slipped out and caught a pass for a touchdown. We lost the game, but I felt like I lost the game because I got beat on that play. That never happened to me again."

Darden recovered quickly from his week one mental lapse. He tied for the team lead in interceptions with three, helping the veteran-laden Browns to a 10–4 record, the AFC's wild card playoff berth, and a near upset of the soon-to-be undefeated Super Bowl champion Miami Dolphins in a divisional playoff game.

Darden moved to free safety the next year and was a staple there for the remainder of his career. After a December tailspin cost the Browns a playoff berth in 1973, some dark days arrived. The team fell to 4–10 in 1974, but Darden was the team leader with eight interceptions. This was also Darden's third and final year returning punts for the Browns (he had done the same in high school and college).

"The early 1970s," Darden said, "was a transitional time for the Browns because most of those guys when I came in were remnants from the '64 championship team. And those guys were pros. They partied hearty, but they worked hard, and they knew the game. They knew where they were supposed to be, when they were supposed to be there. They didn't make too many mental mistakes. I learned a lot being around those guys … Jim Houston, Gene Hickersons, Walt Sumner, Ben Davis."

A knee injury caused Darden to miss the entire 1975 season, which ended in a 3–11 nightmare under first-year head coach Forrest Gregg, who had succeeded Nick Skorich. "The year I was out," Darden said, "I would sit up in the press box area during games because Richie McCabe, our secondary coach, wanted me to be up there by him so we could go over things as they were happening. I learned a lot doing that."

Upon his return in 1976, Darden was in tip-top condition. "Because I was out in '75, I was just ready to play," he said. "That's when I started really becoming a pretty decent player on the pro level."

Becoming a pretty decent player? This from a guy who had eight interceptions just two years earlier? Clearly, Darden's standards were quite lofty.

"I felt I was getting better," he said, "because of my work ethic and feeling more comfortable with what I was supposed to be doing and making the adjustments. I had to make all the adjustment calls for the linebackers and secondary. I was sort of like the quarterback of the defense."

Darden led the Browns with seven interceptions in 1976 as they improved to 9–5 and were in playoff contention through the final weekend. In what was becoming a yearly ritual, Darden once again led the Browns with six picks in 1977, including one returned for a touchdown against the Kansas City Chiefs. The team got off to a fast start, but the bottom fell out in the second half of the season, resulting in a last-place finish and a pink slip for Gregg.

By the time the 1978 season arrived, Sam Rutigliano was the head coach. "Sam was a good teacher," Darden said, "and I enjoyed playing for a coach who taught. Even though he was an offensive-minded coach, he'd also been a secondary coach, so he knew a lot about that area. That endeared him to me, knowing he could watch practice and see something that a guy was doing and come over and correct him and teach him. Sam knew what the player was supposed to be doing, the steps he was supposed to take. So that was always a positive for me."

Darden had his finest season in '78 as his 10 interceptions not only led the Browns—tying him with Tom Colella (1946) and Anthony Henry (2001) for the single-season high in team history —but also led the entire NFL.

"That was quite a thrill," Darden said. "We didn't have too many league leaders on defense back then."

Darden's performance that year earned him All-AFC defensive honors from UPI, *The Sporting News, Pro Football Weekly*, and the Newspaper Enterprise Association. He also was voted to his only Pro Bowl. The Browns won their first three games but wound up 8–8. Then came the fine start in 1979, punctuated by the Monday night rout of the Cowboys and Darden's electrifying pick six. The Kardiac Kids finished 9–7 and barely missed the playoffs. Darden—ho-hum—led the team in interceptions again with five, earning All-AFC defensive acclaim from *Pro Football Weekly* for the second straight season.

"Darden was an outstanding player. For all the troubles the Browns had, they had a couple very good defensive backs through the '70s, and one of them was Thom Darden," said Steve King. "A ball hawk back there is a guy who can obviously turn a game around by getting his hands on the ball and creating turnovers. Darden had that. He had it in college at Michigan, and he had it with the Browns. He was able to affect a lot of games that way. You can't cover receivers all the time. They're going to get open, they're going to make plays, but if you can create enough turnovers, you can make people forget that you got beat on a certain play or you can turn a game around. A team is ready to go in and score, and all of a sudden, you pick off a pass. And Darden did that."

"Thom was a great player, a great personality, and a really good locker room guy," Jerry Sherk said. "He was real key to that defensive backfield."

The 1980 Browns—aka the Kardiac Kids, Chapter Two—were finally able to climb over the Pittsburgh-Houston hump, winning the AFC Central Division with an 11–5 record. A 17–14 upset of the Oilers in the Astrodome on Thanksgiving weekend was perhaps the most crucial win of the season. It not only gave the Browns sole possession of first place, it also fueled a fan reaction of monumental proportions as some 15,000 fans greeted the Browns at Cleveland Hopkins International Airport, causing thousands of dollars' worth of damage upon the team's near midnight arrival that evening.

"The whole concourse was packed!" Darden recalled. "It was both exhilarating and frightening—exhilarating because we'd never had that many people at the airport and frightening because the crowd was just ... I mean, we couldn't get through! Someone took my bag from me! Fortunately, I got it back later. It was just an unbelievable scene!

"The city was just ... it was remarkably exciting to be part of that town during that time. You couldn't go anywhere where our team wasn't the topic of conversation. We felt like rock stars!"

Darden did not lead the Browns in interceptions in 1980. He did, however, return a Jack Thompson pass 23 yards during a 27-24 victory over the Bengals on the final Sunday that clinched the Central Division championship.

Darden possessed great hands—he is the Browns' all-time interceptions leader with 45. "I think a lot more goes into interceptions than just catching the ball," said Mike Peticca. "You have to have preparation, instincts, and knowing how long to watch the quarterback, things like that."

"I loved Thom Darden," said Michael Cuomo. "He was a very underrated safety. Forty-five interceptions? That's ridiculous. He was damn good. He iced a lot of games with fourth-quarter interceptions."

Darden was also known as one of the hardest hitters in the NFL. "He had a punch to him," said King. "Even on those bad teams, he stood out, no question about it. A guy back there who can scare people from coming across the middle … you have to keep your head on a swivel because this guy is going to come up and lay a hit on you. Darden's forte was getting his hands on the ball, but a guy like that who can also deliver a hit is a guy of great value. And a lot of the hits that are illegal now you could do those then, and Darden did them."

"I think Darden was the guy in Cleveland like a guy like Jack Tatum was to Oakland or Mel Blount was to Pittsburgh," Peticca said. "In the hard-hitting category, he was Cleveland's guy who you thought of in those terms. He was Cleveland's guy who was identified in that way, that if you're going over the middle or whatever, Darden was the guy who guys would think of in terms of 'He's around.' He closed on plays really well. He just had such a wide range of area that he would cover. He really anticipated things well. He must've really studied the opponents. He'd be the guy on those Browns teams who maybe receivers would go into a game thinking, 'I've got to be on the lookout for him.' He also had great range as far as being able to cover the intermediate to deep throws. He was a great player."

"He wasn't afraid to throw his body into the fray," said Mike McLain.

Perhaps the most crushing blow Darden ever landed came in that title clincher against the Bengals when he struck Pat McInally so hard, the big receiver actually swallowed his tongue when he hit the ground!

"They had to pull it from his throat," Darden said.

Many say it was a cheap shot. The NFL fined Darden, who saw it differently.

"When McInally [who returned later in the game to make an unbelievable over-the-shoulder touchdown catch] came across the middle, I had to make a decision right then whether I was going for the ball or him," he explained. "Since I couldn't get to the ball in time to intercept, I decided to go for him. I first hit him in his upper chest, but because he was lowering his body my forearm went to his neck. I thought it was a legal hit since I first contacted him in his chest."

Two weeks later came the unfortunate—and infamous—conclusion to the season with the Red Right 88 polar playoff loss to the Oakland Raiders, a game in which Darden traded his cleats for tennis shoes for better footing on a field that, in many areas, was literally a sheet of ice. After the Browns dropped to 5–11 and last place in 1981, they released Darden, who had been struggling with several nagging injuries. He decided to call it quits.

Although he was an education major in college, Darden decided to go a different route. He owned a cable company, worked in the sports management business, and was a security provider before starting The Darden Group, Inc., a consulting business, in 1995, which is still going strong today.

Darden, 74, resides in Cedar Rapids, Iowa, with his wife Melissa. The couple has six grown children—two together and two each from previous marriages. The Dardens also have three grandchildren. As for hobbies, they like to travel.

Darden loved, cherished, playing in front of the Cleveland fans.

"There are none better. They're knowledgeable, they're avid, and they're loyal," he said. "I don't think I could've played anywhere else where the fans would've shown as much love as Cleveland Browns fans showed the Cleveland players. I want to thank those fans for all the years they were in that old stadium cheering for us. Many of those years were lean, but they were still there in great numbers."

Darden did not mince words when asked what it was like to play in Cleveland Stadium.

"It was cold, damp, and nasty," he said, "but it was a thrill to play in that stadium."

Now … The $64,000 Question: Did Ohio State fans back in Sandusky give Darden a hard time when he chose the maize and blue over the scarlet and gray?

"Of course," he laughed. "They still do!"

5

BILLY ANDREWS: MONDAY NIGHT MARVEL

Joe Willie was in town. As in "Broadway Joe" Namath. Nothing more, really, needed to be said. Other than the fact that ABC's very first *Monday Night Football* broadcast was beaming across the land. The Browns were hosting Namath's New York Jets. It was September 21, 1970. All eyes in Cleveland Municipal Stadium were on Broadway Joe, who was known for his perfect spirals, perfect 10s, and perhaps the most famous guarantee of all time. The Browns, though, had a 10-point lead entering the fourth quarter. The Jets cut it to 24–21 with 3:22 remaining on a 33-yard laser from Namath to George Sauer. The Browns were forced to punt on their ensuing possession.

It was anyone's game.

A few minutes later, a backup linebacker by the name of Billy Andrews crashed Broadway Joe's bash. With the Jets on their own 18 yard line and just 47 seconds to go, Namath fired a short pass to the left intended for Emerson Boozer. Andrews dove, intercepted the ball at the 25, got up, turned around, and began running. Rumbling across the field while fending off several would-be tacklers, he crossed the goal line with 35 ticks on the clock.

Game, set, and match, Browns.

Andrews's heroics put the nail in New York's coffin, sealing his team's 31–21 victory, which was played before 85,703 fans, still the largest crowd ever to witness a Browns home game.

"I had man-on-man coverage on Boozer," Andrews said. "Ron Snidow was pressing in on Namath, and Namath threw the ball kind of behind me, and I dove for it and it kind of just stuck in my hand. One of my strong points was coverage because I could backpedal quite well. That was a thrill of a lifetime. It was something you dream about, being in that situation and making that kind of play."

"Billy wasn't the fastest guy in the game," said Fred Hoaglin. "It looked like, 'Oh, they're gonna catch him!' But they didn't. He was able to outrun them."

"Billy Andrews got the most out of his body," Thom Darden said. "He wasn't the fastest guy in the world, but he was smart and he was pretty tough. He was a very capable linebacker. I guess being smart put him in the right position most of the time. And he would hit you."

Andrews's touchdown not only turned out to be his only one in 11 years in the NFL, it changed the course of his career. After being chosen by the Browns in the 13th round of the 1967 NFL-AFL Draft, Andrews had started just four games when he replaced veteran Dale Lindsey at right outside linebacker late in the first half of the Jets game. He stayed there the rest of the night, and after his pick six he remained a starter for the rest of his career.

"After that one play," he said, "I was no longer this guy from a small college who wasn't real big and not real fast. I was a different person in the eyes of the coaches."

Andrews's road to Browns Town began when he was born in Clinton, Louisiana, a town of about 500 people at the time that lies approximately 100 miles northwest of New Orleans. The youngest of three children, he was raised on a farm and attended the same school—yes, the same school—from grades one through twelve.

"We had 13 boys in our senior class," he laughed.

Andrews played baseball, basketball, and football. He even ran track.

"We didn't have a gym for basketball until I was in the ninth grade," he said. "Before that, we played on dirt courts and had to play all our games on the road."

Football, though, was Andrews's true love.

"I'd wanted to play in the NFL from the time I was nine years old," he said.

Andrews, who stood 6-foot, 220 pounds when he was with the Browns, started off as a skinny young kid. "I was small," he said. "I was kind of wormy-like."

His parents, in fact, used to lay awake at night worrying, afraid their son was going to be crushed, broken-hearted, because they believed he would never get to play. "They didn't want to discourage me, though,"

Andrews said. "So it was sort of a tough situation they were in."

Andrews wanted to get bigger, wanted to play football so badly, that he built himself an isometric rack when he was just 12 years old.

"Isometrics," he explained, "is pushing against an immovable object. In other words, with the exercise I did, you lay on the bench and do a bench press, but it doesn't move. You're straining as hard as you can to push against it. I'd stick a weight bar through holes that I'd drilled in a four-by-four, and it was in concrete in the ground that I'd placed there. I'd be pushing against it as hard as I could, but it wouldn't move. It was a way I could do lifts without weights to try to get stronger than what I could get even with weights. It built tremendous strength, but it can make your muscles stronger than the tendons could stand, so I had to be careful."

When his father saw that young Billy was serious about weight training, he began driving him three times a week to a weightlifting studio in Baton Rouge, about 45 minutes away, owned by the renowned Alvin Roy. Roy had been an Olympic trainer and eventually became the first strength coach of a professional football team, the 1963 San Diego Chargers, and four more pro football teams in the years to come.

"My dad, both of my parents actually, wanted me to have every opportunity to do what my dream was, and that was to play football," Andrews said. "Even though

I was getting bigger from the isometrics, I really didn't know what I was doing. But this guy, Alvin Roy, was so far ahead of his time in weightlifting. He had all the techniques and everything."

At every level of football, Andrews would run into the same problem—the coaches would tell him he couldn't play, that he wasn't big enough, strong enough, or fast enough. "But at every level I was able to overcome," he said, "and I'd say a lot of it was due to Alvin Roy's training and a drive I had that I wasn't going to be told, 'No.'"

Andrews continued training at Roy's studio through high school, during the summers in college, and even in the offseason when he was in the pros, joining LSU and NFL stars Jim Taylor and Billy Cannon.

"That's how I was stronger than a lot of players," he said. "I was muscled up but not ripped with a lot of bulk. I had strong muscles."

Andrews also possessed lots of strength—especially in his hands—from years of working on the family farm. "If I was throwing square bales of hay," he said, "I'd do it like I was forearming somebody. Everything was centered around my making it in football."

Andrews, who eventually maxed out at 400 pounds on the bench press while with the Browns, played both center and linebacker from his early days all the way through high school and on into his time at Southeastern Louisiana College (now Southeastern Louisiana University). He made All-State as a senior in high school in helping his team to a state championship, and had two interceptions in the title game.

Besides Southeastern Louisiana, the only other college that showed interest in Andrews was LSU.

"But LSU's defensive coach, John North, told me I was too small," he said. "I weighed all of 160 pounds then."

By the time the Louisiana High School All-Star Game came around the summer after Andrews graduated, North and LSU were singing a different tune. The reason? Andrews's stellar performance in the game—in which he competed against several LSU recruits—included an interception and several tackles.

"I guess that got their attention," Andrews laughed. "I was also up to 185 pounds by then. North came up to me afterwards and asked me if I'd consider accepting a full scholarship to LSU. I wasn't too small anymore apparently."

Andrews declined because he had already accepted a full ride to play at Southeastern Louisiana, which lies some 50 miles from Clinton.

"Even though LSU was big-time and had won a national title in 1958," he said, "my dad was very adamant that 'wherever you sign is where you're going.'"

That's how Andrews wound up at Southeastern Louisiana, where he started at linebacker and part-time at center as a freshman for the Lions. Other than during an injury-plagued senior year, he was a starter at both positions for the remainder of his college career.

Andrews, who majored in animal science but never pursued that path, desperately wanted to be drafted by his home-state team, the expansion New Orleans Saints, in the 1967 NFL-AFL Draft. He soon realized, however, it would have been a horrible situation if he had. Translation: It took the Saints 21 years to field a winning team.

Instead, Andrews was drafted by the Browns, one of the most successful franchises of the time. He recalled an amusing side note from the day he was drafted. "About 30 minutes after the Browns called to tell me they'd picked me," he said, "the Steelers called and said they wanted to sign me as a free agent since I'd gone undrafted."

Huh? Andrews *had* been drafted—by the Browns!

"Immediately," he laughed, "I thought one of my good friends had played a prank on me when I'd gotten the call from the Browns, pretending to be someone from the Browns. To this day, I don't understand why the Steelers thought I hadn't been drafted."

Andrews made the long drive from Clinton to Hiram in the summer of '67 for his first Browns training camp. He gave it his all but was not 100 percent sure he would make the already linebacker-rich roster until the final cut. "I wanted to play so badly," he said, "that I would've probably paid the Browns to let me play."

After his memorable interception return against the Jets in 1970, Andrews immediately became the Browns' starting right outside linebacker. He stayed there for three years, helping his team to playoff appearances in 1971 and 1972. He intercepted a pair of Jim Plunkett passes in a 1971 game against New England on the way to winning the Cleveland Touchdown Club Defensive Player of the Year award.

"That game against the Patriots was quite a thrill," he said. "Plunkett had won the Heisman Trophy the year before."

Andrews was moved to middle linebacker in 1973 and was named the defensive captain. Unfortunately, he ruptured a disc in his back early that year, forcing surgery and causing him to miss most of the season. He attempted a comeback in 1974, but recurring effects from the injury limited him to a reserve role at all three linebacker positions. He asked the Browns to trade him after the season.

"I wasn't interested in being a backup," he said.

The Browns granted Andrews his wish. They traded him to Denver, but the Broncos wanted him to be their backup middle linebacker. "Again, I didn't want to be a backup," he said, "and I wasn't a middle linebacker. I had only played in the middle those few games in '73."

Andrews, who also contributed on the special teams throughout his career, wound up in San Diego and was the Chargers' starting left outside linebacker in 1975. He started at the same position for the Kansas City Chiefs in 1976 and 1977. One play he will never forget while he was with the Chiefs took place against the Browns in the

'76 season finale at Arrowhead Stadium. Andrews was on special teams and somehow a punt by Don Cockroft ended up in in his hands. "I returned the ball about 70 yards before Don tackled me at the 2 yard line," he recalled.

Andrews, who retired after the 1977 season, is as humble as they come. He feels blessed to have been born with what he calls "football smarts."

"When I looked at myself and what I could do back then," he said, "you couldn't measure by clock times and things like that. You could only measure it by what I could do on the field. What I had was hard to measure."

Andrews possessed the innate ability to read a play and be off and running before other linebackers, who may have been faster than him, even moved.

"That's how I made up for my lack of speed," he said.

After retiring, Andrews dabbled in teaching and coaching – football *and* basketball – at the high school level for a while before building, and running, his own dairy farm for more than 25 years. He also owned his own hay business before retiring in 2018. He resides in Clinton with his wife of 60 years, Kay, his high school sweetheart. The couple has two grown daughters, a grown son, and six grandchildren. Son Will took after Dad and played linebacker in college, including two years backing up Takeo Spikes at Auburn University.

In his spare time Andrews, 79, enjoys his family, hunting, Christian fellowship, and preaching.

"We try to get up to Cleveland as much as possible," he said. "They—the old Browns and the new Browns—have always treated me and my family like we're royalty, and we're just plain, old, simple country people."

Even after all these years have passed since his historic interception on that balmy night in 1970, Andrews remains in disbelief at how big a phenomenon Monday Night Football became.

"Nobody at that point in time," he said, "really thought Monday Night Football would amount to anything. Most people thought it was going to fail. In fact, my family back in Clinton had to drive 55 miles and get a hotel room to watch that Jets game because the local ABC affiliate chose not to show it. I even remember my teammates and I were kind of aggravated that we didn't get to play on Sunday. We had to change our 'time clocks,' if you will, from playing a day game on Sunday to playing a night game on a Monday. We were all saying, 'Here we are playing on Monday night way after all the other teams had played, and we're also gonna have to come back and play again six days later.'"

"A guy comes out of nowhere, Billy Andrews, and he makes the play of the game," Steve King said. "Billy Andrews is at one end of the spectrum, Joe Willie Namath is at the other. Billy Andrews read it, picked it off, ran it in for a touchdown. It started a precedence that lasted for years of guys coming out of nowhere and becoming the hero on Monday Night Football. It was Walter Mitty. All of a sudden, these guys come out of nowhere. And Billy Andrews started that. I remember asking Andrews, 'Do you ever think about that game?' He said, 'Only every day.' That pick six changed his life. It was just a little get-some-yardage play. They were coming with the rush, and they just threw the ball out there. Namath never saw it. And he just ran it in. It was what *Monday Night Football* needed. They couldn't have a 10–7 game. If that game had been a dud, the naysayers would've said, 'See, I told you so. It was a stupid idea.' There wasn't anything about that game that wasn't perfect.

"After the Namaths and the Bill Nelsens and the Leroy Kellys and the Emerson Boozers and all these guys who had big names, how are we going to decide this? Billy Andrews. Who the heck is Billy Andrews? It changed television, it changed the game, it changed the National Football League, and it change the guy's life. One game. The areas in which the game went into, the ratings were off the charts. And it didn't take long for all those affiliates that said no initially to say yes.

"The expectations for football on Monday night were … well … it was an experiment, a gamble," said Andrews. "But the kind of game we had that night, an exciting game that had Joe Namath, a huge crowd, and several big plays kind of set it off, gave *Monday Night Football* a good start."

And a defensive gem that evening by Billy Andrews was the lighter fluid behind the rocket launch.

6

CLOSE BUT NO CIGAR: A NEAR UPSET IN THE ORANGE BOWL

The Browns nearly pulled of a shocker on Christmas Eve 1972 against the Miami Dolphins in front of an Orange Bowl sellout crowd of 80,010. The Dolphins finished 14–0 during the regular season and were aiming to become the first team in NFL history to go undefeated and untied for an entire season (including the postseason) and the first team overall in pro football since 1948 when, ironically, the Browns themselves did it while a member of the All-America Football Conference. The Browns, meanwhile, finished 10–4 and the AFC's wild-card team. They were heavy underdogs in this AFC divisional playoff.

"I was so excited to get to play the Dolphins, to get to play against Paul Warfield, who I had practiced against so many times over the years before he went to Miami," Billy Andrews remembered. "My best friend when he was with Cleveland was Bob Matheson. To get to play against him was exciting."

The visitors got off to a poor start when a Don Cockroft punt deep in Browns territory was blocked due in large part to a bad snap by Fred Hoaglin and returned five yards for a touchdown by Charlie Baab for a 7–0 Dolphins lead. "We lost that game because of the blocked punt," Jim Houston recalled. "I was the quarterback on the punting team, and for some reason, a couple guys got in there. That did us in."

A 40-yard field goal by Garo Yepremian gave the home team a 10–0 first-quarter lead that stood until halftime. The Browns got on the board in the third quarter, making the score 10–7 on a five-yard touchdown run by quarterback Mike Phipps. Yepremian's 46-yard field goal in the fourth quarter upped the Dolphins' lead to 13-7. With 8:11 to go in the game, the Browns shocked the world by forging ahead, 14–13, when Phipps hit Fair Hooker on a 27-yard touchdown pass. Hooker cut into the middle of the field and then cut out, and there was nobody there. Phipps lofted him the ball. Miami would not be deterred, however, and marched right down the field for what turned out to be the winning score, an eight-yard run by Jim Kiick. Miami won, 20–14.

"That game is still in my head. We had those guys beat," Thom Darden said. "There was no reason for us not to win that game. They called a pass interference penalty on Billy Andrews, who was covering Paul Warfield when we were up 14–13 in the fourth quarter. I'll never forget that. The Dolphins were in third-and-long, and that pass interference call got them out of trouble, got them into our territory, and it just seemed like it took the wind out of our sails. I think it was a bad call. It wasn't like Billy twisted Warfield or anything, it was incidental contact, I think. Had that penalty not been called, we would've won the game because if that play doesn't go, they have to punt the ball or try desperately to get a first down."

"I still dispute that call," Andrews said.

Steve King remembered a 35-yard pass from Earl Morrall to Warfield on a post pattern down the middle on the Dolphins' winning drive. "It was ironic, it seemed fitting," said King. "Who did Warfield beat but Ben Davis, the guy he practiced against for all those years?"

It was a heartbreaking defeat for the Browns. Not only was it remarkable that they came so close to winning the game and advancing to the AFC Championship Game, even more amazing was that they did it despite five interceptions by Phipps. "I think our offensive line might've led the team in tackles," Doug Dieken laughed. "Having played at Illinois and having gone 4–26 in three years there, just the fact that we won 10 games in the season was kind of like *Fantasy Island*. We could've put a little smudge in Don Shula's perfect season. You don't think about the five interceptions until the game is over and you say, 'How the hell did we lose *that*?'"

"You obviously did not like the interceptions," Mike Peticca said, "but that was an era of the interception. You're going against a great defense. But the Browns' defense was amazing that game. You've got Larry Csonka, Jim Kiick, and Mercury Morris. You had Paul Warfield,

Howard Twilley, and Jim Mandich and a terrific offensive line. The No-Name Defense was really good, and the fact that the Browns moved the ball a couple times for touchdowns was impressive, but the Browns' defense was really impressive. You had Bob Briggs, Jerry Sherk was becoming one of the best tackles in the league. He and Walter Johnson were at the time as good as any tackle duo in the league. Houston, in his last game, had a good game. There was something about the way the Browns' defense was playing, you just thought they were in the game."

"We played them very well," said Darden. "We should've beaten them. I think we outplayed them."

"We went toe to toe with them," Jerry Sherk said. "I darted through the line one time, and I hit Csonka behind the line. I got him at his knees, and he went down. I thought, 'Well, this is the great Larry Csonka, and I brought him down pretty easily.' To qualify that, he was a guy who, if he got a head of steam, and he did the same thing, he'd probably run right over you. I just hit him at the right point."

"The Dolphins were trying to run the ball, and I can remember Walter Johnson was just lights out in the middle. They stacked up the middle, and Kiick and Csonka and Morris just couldn't run," King remembered. "The Browns were very close to upsetting the Dolphins. They had the game won."

"The Browns' defense was so scrappy," said Michael

Cuomo. "They did a good job against Miami in the running game."

"We outplayed them all over the field," said Andrews.

Added Dan Coughlin, "They damn near beat 'em."

7

CLAY AND OZZIE IN THE SAME DRAFT? BOTH IN THE FIRST ROUND? WOW!

The best draft class the Browns had in the 1970s was the 1978 edition when they selected Ozzie Newsome and Clay Matthews, the former a Hall of Famer and the latter a should-be Hall of Famer, in the first round. Matthews was the 12th pick overall, and Newsome was the 23rd choice overall. Newsome, a wide receiver at the University of Alabama who was switched to tight end in Cleveland, was known as "The Wizard of Oz" for his remarkable catches. He led the Browns in receptions and receiving yards every season from 1981 to 1985 and led the team in touchdown receptions in 1979, 1981, and from 1983 to 1985. Newsome's 1,002 yards receiving in 1981 were the most by a Brown in 13 years. He totaled a team-record 89 catches in both 1983 and 1984. He had 191 receiving yards against the New York Jets on October 14, 1984.

Newsome's career totals of 662 receptions and 7,980 receiving yards rank first in Browns annals. His 114 receiving yards in Cleveland's thrilling 23–20 double-overtime win over the Jets in an AFC divisional playoff on January 3, 1987, landed him on the cover of *Sports Illustrated*. Newsome was a Pro Bowler in 1981, 1984, and 1985. He was inducted into the Pro Football Hall of Fame in 1999.

Sam Rutigliano explained why he turned Newsome into a tight end. "It gave Ozzie an opportunity to block linebackers," he said. "We never asked him to block defensive ends, but playing him at tight end opened the door for Reggie [Rucker], opened the door for [Dave] Logan, opened the door for the running backs, because every game we played, the defense was trying to defend Ozzie."

"[Browns tight ends/wide receivers coach] Rich Kotite came down [to Alabama] to work [eventual Browns teammate] Johnny Davis and I out," Newsome recalled. "Johnny went over and worked out, and he came back and told me, 'Hey man, the coach from the Browns said he just wants you to come over and catch two or three passes, he's not going to put you through an extensive workout. So I went over, and Rich worked me out and, like Johnny said, he only threw me four or five passes, but what he wanted to see was my lower body, to see if my lower body would handle the weight gain if I was to put it on my upper body so they could talk about moving me to tight end. I didn't know that at the time, but he wanted to eyeball me [for a switch to tight end].

"In the draft Wes Chandler goes, James Lofton goes,

Ken MacAfee goes, and John Jefferson goes. We were all, 'Whose gonna be first, second, third, and all of that?' And then Cleveland traded the choice back two picks, and at that point I was like, 'Well, whatever is gonna happen is gonna happen,' and by the time I could get that out of my mouth, I got a call from Art [Modell] and Sam.

"Throughout the draft process, I think it was 50-50 about the teams that I had talked to. Some were saying they would let me stay at wide receiver, others were asking me if I would consider a move to tight end. I went through my first mini-camp as a wide receiver. And it was interesting that the week that they had the rookie mini-camp I called Sam and said, 'You know, I'd like to not participate in that because that's the week of graduation, and my family wants to see me graduate. He allowed me to do that. So I went in with the veterans the following week. I was the only rookie who was at the veteran camp. And those three days I worked at wide receiver. But they wanted to keep some guys for an additional three or four days, and I was one of them. At that point, Kotite told me that Sam wanted to see me. And I said, 'Okay.' But Sam was not there when I went to see him, so I went back to Rich and said, 'Well, do you know what he wants to see me about?' He said, 'Yeah, he wants to see you about moving to tight end.'

"The next day I met with Sam, and he said, 'You know, you could be a good receiver in this league, there's no doubt. You just proved that over the last three days of this mini-camp. But we think you could be a *great* tight end. And we're going to move you to tight end with your willingness, but if we're going to move you, we're going to throw you the football. We're going to throw you a lot of footballs at tight end.' And he was very honest and very truthful, and that's what they did, and that's how I accepted the move.

"My personal preference was catching the football … because I had played in a wishbone [in college], and so you weren't getting but three or four passes a day, so blocking was not a problem. It wasn't until the *real* training camp that Rich told me what he came down [to Alabama] for. I did not know at that point. I thought he was just coming to work me out as a receiver. But he told me at that point during training camp that that's what he was looking at."

Oh, another thing. Newsome could catch the ball.

"He dropped one pass in the six-and-a-half years I was with him," Rutigliano said in awe.

"Kellen Winslow gets all the glory, but he wasn't drafted until '79," Steve King said. "The guy who changed how the game was played was Ozzie because Sam realized he was big enough to run down the field and make plays as a tight end in a wide receiver's body. He was too big for corners to cover, and he was too fast for safeties. He really became another wide receiver. Milt Morin and Mike Ditka were great tight ends, but they were guys who would run seven-yard curl routes, and they would catch the ball and just fall down. Who would've thought a guy coming out of a wishbone offense in college would be a prolific pass catcher? Using Ozzie like a wide receiver … no one had ever seen anything like that before. A tight end running down the field making plays? That changed the game. It took a lot of teams to catch up to that. All these tight ends now who are making plays down the field? That all started with Ozzie Newsome."

Matthews, a linebacker from the University of Southern California, not only had physical talents but also amazing durability. He played for Cleveland from 1978 to 1993. If his level of play tailed off at all late in his long career with the Browns, it wasn't by much. His 12 sacks in 1984 ranked second on the team. His nine sacks in 1992 tied for the team lead. Matthews was a Pro Bowler in 1985 and from 1987 to 1989.

"I think Matthews should be in the Hall of Fame, there's no question in my mind," said King. "Matthews … who's this guy? A linebacker from USC. He got hurt in the preseason or training camp in '78. I think it was an ankle problem. You never would've thought that guy would become an iron man."

Clay Matthews in action against Seattle, November 11, 1979
*The Cleveland Press Collection, Michael Schwartz Library,
Cleveland State University*

The Browns chose kickoff returner Keith Wright from
Memphis State University (now Memphis University) in
the fifth round. Wright led Cleveland in kickoff return
yards in 1978 and returned the opening kickoff 86 yards
against the Chiefs on October 22 that year. He also
returned punts and led the team in punt returns and
punt return yardage in 1978 and 1980. Wright was voted
to the All-AFC offensive team in 1978 by *Pro Football*

Weekly. The Browns selected punter Johnny Evans in the second round out of North Carolina State. Evans's 8,463 punting yards rank 10th all-time for the Browns. The Browns also chose running back Larry Collins from Texas A&M University-Kingsville and quarterback Mark Miller from Bowling Green State University in the third round plus defensive tackle Jesse Turnbow out of the University of Tennessee in the eighth round. Miller spent the 1978 and 1979 seasons with Cleveland, and Collins and Turnbow spent the 1978 season with the team.

"That," said King, "was the third-best draft the Browns ever had behind only the 1957 and 1964 drafts. It was a bonanza."

Another great draft class of the 1970s was the 1971 edition when the Browns selected wide receiver/tight end Doug Dieken from the University of Illinois in the sixth round. Cleveland switched Dieken to offensive left tackle, and he carried on the fine tradition of Browns left tackles when he replaced veteran Dick Schafrath during the 1971 season. One of Dieken's more memorable moments, though, came as a receiver when, on October 30, 1983, at home against the Oilers, he caught a 14-yard touchdown pass from Paul McDonald on a fake field goal for the only touchdown of his career. Dieken was a Pro Bowler in 1980.

"You've got the left tackles in team history," King said, "the Joe Thomases, the Schafraths, and the Lou Grozas, all of those guys … and then there's Dieken who's just a step down and is part of that lineage of great left tackles."

The Browns that year also drafted defensive back Clarence Scott from Kansas State University in the first round and linebacker Charlie Hall out of the University of Houston in the third round. Scott, who played mainly left cornerback and strong safety, led the Browns in interceptions in 1973 and 1981. His 39 career picks rank third all-time in team history. In 1973 he was named to the All-AFC defensive team by United Press International and was a Pro Bowler. Meanwhile, Hall tied for the team lead in interceptions in 1975. One memorable theft occurred on November 4, 1979, when with Philadelphia at the Browns' 1 yard line, he picked off Ron Jaworski with no time left, preserving the Browns' 24–19 victory. Hall had 13 interceptions in his career.

"Clarence Scott doesn't get the credit for how good of a cornerback he was because the teams weren't very good," said King. "Charlie Hall was a tremendous outside linebacker. He was solid, solid, solid."

The Browns picked six other players in 1971 who spent minimal time with the team during the 1971 and 1972 seasons.

The Browns' 1976 draft class was a fine one, too, led by first-round pick Mike Pruitt, a fullback from Purdue University, third-round selection Dave Logan, a wide receiver from the University of Colorado, and fifth-round pick Henry Sheppard, an offensive lineman from Southern

Methodist University. Pruitt was a benchwarmer for the most part until new head coach Rutigliano gave him his shot in 1978. Pruitt exploded for a 71-yard touchdown run against the Bills on October 29 of that year, and that catapulted him to some serious success during the next five seasons. He was the team leader in rushing yards every season from 1979 to 1983, surpassing 1,000 yards every season except the strike-shortened year of 1982. Pruitt's 6,540 rushing yards rank third all-time for the Browns. He could also catch the ball, improving in that category greatly later in his career as his 63 receptions in both 1980 and 1981 attested. He was picked for the Pro Bowl in 1979 and 1980.

Logan was a three-sport star in college and used his height and angular build to produce some stellar seasons with the Browns. He was the team leader in receptions and receiving yards in 1979 and receiving yards in 1980. Logan totaled 262 receptions and 24 touchdown catches in his Browns career, many of them coming in spectacular fashion that only someone with his gifted athletic abilities could have carried out. "Dave might be one of the best athletes I ever played with. He was a great competitor," Dieken said. "He was drafted by the NFL, Major League Baseball, and the NBA."

Dave Logan scores on a 35-yard pass play from Brian Sipe against Baltimore, September 16, 1979

The Cleveland Press Collection, Michael Schwartz Library, Cleveland State University

Sheppard, meanwhile, was a fine player who started most of his career and was a part of the Kardiac Kids offensive line that protected Brian Sipe as if he were a newborn baby. The Browns also drafted defensive end Mike St. Clair in 1976 in the fourth round from Grambling State University. Although not a starter, St. Clair was a solid backup for the Browns.

"When you saw the draft in 1976 and what it was at

the end of the '76 season and even at the end of the '77 season, you didn't look at that draft the same way you did later," said King. "Pruitt had fumbling problems and bad hands and got in Forrest Gregg's doghouse. You had this great runner who they thought they had, he had to develop. Dave Logan, he caught 24 passes in two years as a tight end. He wasn't a tight end, he was a wide receiver. Sam said when he called all the players after he got the job, he called Logan and told him he was going to change him from tight end to wide receiver and he'd put Ozzie at tight end, and he thought Logan was going to reach through the phone and kiss him. You didn't see that until 1978. Mike St. Clair was a pass rusher. It gave them two pass rushers—St. Clair and Joe Jones. They thought they had the two defensive ends for the future. Then in 1978 Pruitt started to come around, and Dave Logan started to make plays."

The 1970 draft was a good one, too. The gem was no doubt right defensive tackle Jerry Sherk, who the Browns selected in the second round out of Oklahoma State University. Sherk started every game from 1970 to 1976. He was first-team All-Pro and was the Newspaper Enterprise Association's NFL Defensive Player of the Year in 1976. He was a Pro Bowler from 1973 through 1976. A staph infection suffered during a game in Philadelphia on November 4, 1979, not only, for all intents and purposes, ended his career, it almost cost him a leg and even his life. Many say, had Sherk not suffered that staph infection and played two or three more healthy seasons, he would have been a sure Hall of Famer.

"I think Sherk is the greatest defensive tackle in the history of the team," said King. "As good as Walter Johnson was, Sherk was better. Sherk was better than Bob Gain. Sherk was better than Don Colo. As a middle interior player, there was no question the best one was Jerry Sherk. Think about this. How much better would the 1980 Browns have been had Jerry Sherk been able to play? How much better would that defense have been because Marty [Schottenheimer] came in as defensive coordinator that year? Sherk would've been a terror in 1980."

Also in the second round in 1970, the Browns chose defensive end Joe "Turkey" Jones out of Tennessee State University. Jones started most of the games in his Browns career from 1970 to 1973 and 1975 to 1978. He was a talented player but will always be remembered for sacking Pittsburgh's Terry Bradshaw and slamming him head first to the ground in a home game on October 10, 1976. Late in the first round, the Browns chose offensive lineman Bob McKay from the University of Texas. McKay started most of the games in his Browns career that lasted from 1970 to 1975.

The 1970 draft also brought quarterback Mike Phipps from Purdue University with the third overall pick. Although he had his moments, there simply were not enough of them. His best season with Cleveland was in 1972 when he threw for nearly 2,000 yards with 13 touchdown passes and 16 interceptions in leading the Browns to a playoff berth. Through his final season with Cleveland in 1976, Phipps completed a bit more than 48 percent of his passes and had 40 touchdown passes and 81 interceptions.

The 1972 draft produced a shiny diamond in the rough—quarterback Brian Sipe in the 13th round out of San Diego State University. After spending his first two years on the practice squad, Sipe joined the regular roster in 1974 and backed up Phipps until replacing him two years later when Phipps was injured. Sipe was the leader of the Kardiac Kids in 1979 and 1980, the latter season in which, among several awards he won, was named the NFL's Player of the Year by the Associated Press in passing for 4,132 yards and 30 touchdowns, both of which are still team records, and just 14 interceptions in leading his team to the AFC Central Division title. Sipe, who played for the Browns through 1983, remains the Browns' all-time leader in passing yards with 23,713.

"In what world – certainly not the NFL today – would you draft a player in 1972 and him not making a name for himself heading into the 1978 season would he have been still on the roster?" said King. "That would never happen today. Sipe stuck with it. Sam had that offensive mind, and he and [quarterbacks coach] Jim Shofner bonded. It was the perfect storm, and Sipe took advantage of that. He finally got the want-to. Football had been just something: 'I'll be okay at it.' He never really had a heart for it. And all of a sudden Sam came in and gave him that heart and that drive, that inspiration to develop into a good player, and he stuck with him. He stuck with him all the way until almost the end of the season in '78, and he still hadn't done anything. He was convinced that Sipe could be that leader, could be that player, he was convinced of it. Sipe had been a catcher on a Little League World Series champion, and Sam said a guy who could be a catcher had to be a leader, and that leadership was within him. He knew Sipe had that winning edge. When the situation got tight, he played his best football."

Cleveland's first-round pick in the 1972 draft was free safety Thom Darden from the University of Michigan. Darden not only was a hard hitter, he had good hands as evidenced by his team-record 45 overall interceptions in his career that lasted from 1972 to 1974 and 1976 to 1981. He led the entire NFL with 10 interceptions in 1978, his lone Pro Bowl year, and he had eight picks in 1974.

"It's the safety's job to make hits and be a ball hawk, and nobody did it better than Thom Darden," said King. "For all those bad teams the Browns had, he and Clarence Scott were two Pro Bowl–caliber players in the defensive backfield. They just didn't have enough players around them. Darden was a tremendous player. Forty-five interceptions? That was great. A lot of times, those interceptions didn't amount to points because you had bad offenses for a lot of that time. Darden made big hits. He was prolific in '74, had the knee injury in '75, and came right back and was prolific in '76. That knee injury … it was like it didn't happen. That was huge. He was a great player, great hands, had a nose for the football."

The Browns also selected running back Hugh McKinnis and kick return man Billy Lefear in the eighth and ninth rounds, respectively, in 1972. McKinnis, a spot starter, played for Cleveland form 1973 to 1975, his best season coming in 1974 when he rushed for 519 yards and two touchdowns and caught 32 passes for 258 yards. Lefear, who played from 1972 to 1975, was a decent return man. He had a 92-yard kickoff return against the Bengals on November 23, 1975.

8

GREG PRUITT: I'M IN THE WRONG LOCKER ROOM!

It was Greg Pruitt's rookie year of 1973, the Sunday after Thanksgiving. The former University of Oklahoma speedster had just dashed 19 yards for a touchdown with less than a minute to go in the game to give the Browns a 21–16 lead over bitter rival Pittsburgh. The Browns went on to win, pulling within half a game of the AFC Central Division-leading Steelers. Nearly 70,000 fans in Cleveland Municipal Stadium erupted in pandemonium. Thousands of them rushed the field as Pruitt, the little rookie halfback, was engulfed in a sea of worshippers. Some fans even tried to tear down the goalposts.

"You would've thought we just won a championship," Pruitt recalled. "It was then that I realized just what the rivalry with the Steelers means to Browns fans, how important it is. It was really something, the way those fans went crazy. It reminded me of my days at Oklahoma, where football is like a religion. I had thousands of people hitting me, slapping me, on the helmet. It was nuts!"

Pruitt had one thing on his mind—to get to the safe environs of the locker room. "I was able to get to the dugout and into the locker room," he said. "I figured once I got into the locker room, there would be a whole lot of press and media people wanting to interview me and ask me questions. So while I was walking to the locker room, I was planning out what I was going to say."

Pruitt got so turned around that he made a shocking discovery as he entered the locker room.

"It was the Pittsburgh Steelers locker room!" he exclaimed. "I went to the wrong locker room! Right as I opened the door, Chuck Noll was screaming at his players. When I walked in, it got so quiet, you could hear a pin drop."

There was Pruitt, this rookie who had scored the winning touchdown to beat the Steelers minutes earlier, standing there with forty-five angry, black jersey-clad Pittsburgh Steelers staring at him. "I got out of there pretty fast," said Pruitt, who headed back toward the field. "The fans were still out there, though. On one end of the tunnel were thousands of fans going berserk, and on the other end was the Pittsburgh Steelers' locker room. I was stuck! So I just stood in the tunnel, waiting for the fans to leave."

By the time Pruitt made his way across the field to the Browns locker room, the press was long gone. His planned remarks went for naught as his exciting day concluded quietly.

Towards the end of that 1973 Steelers game,

Pruitt made a spectacular play that set up his winning touchdown run.

"It was a 42-yard pass play from Mike Phipps," Steve King said. "He dodged about eight Steelers. It was incredible. I know Jim Brown had some amazing runs, but that play that Pruitt made was as good as anything Brown did and anything Bobby Mitchell did. They couldn't tackle him, they couldn't grab him. You tried to get him, he'd slip out of your hands. They couldn't touch him. It almost looked like it was staged. Pruitt had some muscle, some bulk in his upper body, so he could break tackles. Glen Edwards might've missed him twice. I was sitting in the bleachers with my father. It was third-and-9, so Pittsburgh brings the house. They rushed Phipps and forced him to the right. And you could see from the bleachers that Pruitt was wide open maybe 18, 19 yards downfield right in front of the Pittsburgh bench. Phipps finally saw him and threw the ball to him, and Pruitt got the ball, took a jab step toward the Pittsburgh bench, then he looked back running almost like a semi-circle back to get an angle, headed toward the Browns bench, and then cut down the sideline. It was as good of a play as a Cleveland Browns player has ever made. That, to me, was the greatest single play I've ever seen."

Pruitt's rookie season included several other thrilling moments. On October 28 he scored on a spectacular run against the Chargers late in the game in which he altered his path while trapped in the backfield. It went in the books as a seven-yard run, but it seemed as if Pruitt ran 50 yards to do it. Two weeks later he burst down the right sideline for a 53-yard touchdown run that helped defeat the Oilers. On December 2, Pruitt sped down the right sideline again for a 65-yard score that helped tie Kansas City and keep Cleveland's playoff hopes alive and well. Unfortunately, the Browns fizzled at the end and lost their last two games, denying them a postseason berth.

Some seven months before the 1973 season began, on the day of the NFL draft, the Cleveland Browns were the last thing on Pruitt's mind. He was sure he was headed to New England. "Chuck Fairbanks was the new head coach up there," Pruitt recalled. "He was the head coach at Oklahoma the year before when I was there. The Patriots had three first-round picks. I thought for sure they'd take me in the first round."

Not only did New England not select Pruitt in the first round, nobody did. "I was shocked," he admitted. "I thought for sure I'd go to New England, and for sure that I'd go in the first round. I mean, I finished second in the Heisman Trophy voting!"

Pruitt thinks his size—5-foot-10, 186 pounds— caused the fall. "I don't know what else it could've been," he said.

Pruitt enjoyed a stellar career at Oklahoma, gaining nearly 1,800 yards rushing and scoring 18 touchdowns on the ground his junior year in 1971. He rushed for more than 1,000 yards and scored 13 rushing touchdowns as a senior. He led the Sooners to two 11–1 records, two Sugar Bowl wins, and a pair of Associated Press number two rankings in 1971 and 1972. The Sooners' lone defeat in '71 came at the hands of Nebraska, a 35–31 thriller that has been dubbed "The Game of the Century."

"I covered that Oklahoma-Nebraska game," Dan Coughlin said. "At that time, that was the greatest football game I had ever seen at any level, and Pruitt was fantastic in that game."

"I saw him play in the Sugar Bowl when I was a kid," said Mike McLain. "My mom was from New Orleans, so we used to go down there and visit every year, so I went to a bunch of Sugar Bowls."

When the first round of the 1973 NFL draft came to a close, Pruitt left for the links. "I decided to go play golf," he said. "And I hate golf, always have. But I just needed to get away from all the hoopla and the press, so I went and hid on the golf course."

That is where Pruitt received the news that the Browns had drafted him. They chose him in the second round with the 30th overall pick.

"I was excited when the Browns got him," McLain said.

Pruitt recognized that the Browns had a strong running back tradition. In fact, when he was growing up in Houston, he and his friends would watch on television highlights of Jim Brown, then try to emulate him in their pickup games.

"One day," Pruitt said, "a kid named Charles Law

was running around left end and could've gone for a touchdown. But on TV he'd seen Jim Brown run to the left and then cut to the right and score on an amazing play. So the kid tried that. He could've scored easily had he stayed to the left, but instead he wanted to be Jim Brown. He cut back to the right and ended up with two broken legs, a broken right arm, and a bruised sternum."

Pruitt admitted he arrived in Cleveland as a cocky rookie who thought he knew it all. Leroy Kelly set him straight. "At first I thought to myself, 'I finished second in the Heisman voting, I'm just as good as Leroy Kelly and any other back here,'" said Pruitt. "But soon I realized Leroy had been in the pros a long time and knew a whole lot more than me, like some of the intricacies of the game. I started to listen to him."

That was a smart move as Pruitt's second-half surge his rookie season attested. He finished third on the Browns in rushing yards and second with four rushing touchdowns. He led the team in rushing yards the next five years. In 1975 he became the main man by rushing for 1,067 yards, the first of three straight 1,000-yard seasons. He nearly made it four straight, falling just short in 1978 with 960 yards.

Pruitt's running style never allowed defenders to get straight hits on him. "I always was kind of shifty," he said. "I would never try to be physical with a guy or take a guy on. I would always try to fake a guy. I'd only be physical if I had to be because of my size."

Pruitt's famed tearaway jersey didn't hurt. Defenders already had a hard enough time catching the little "water bug," as Howard Cosell called him. The tearaway jersey, made of delicate material that would tear easily when defenders grabbed it, allowed Pruitt to gain a few extra yards here and there. The tearaway seemed to be an "unwritten" rules infraction but not enforced at the time—until it was banned in 1979. After a time, however, those jerseys became more trouble than they were worth.

"I personally did not like the tearaway," Pruitt said. "More and more people realized that I wore it and understood that I played a big part of the offense, that I was a primary receiver, or primary person, that the Browns went to in key situations, and they would just tear my jersey off and tell the referee. I'd have to leave the field to put a new jersey on. So I found myself running to and from the sideline more than I liked, and I couldn't really get into the flow of the game.

"One time, before a game with the Dallas Cowboys, I was walking out of the tunnel with [Cowboys receiver] Bob Hayes. He said, 'Hey, is that a tearaway you got on?' He walked up and tore it off! And he said, 'Oh, I guess it is.' I had to turn around and go back to the locker room and change my jersey.

"It enhanced my style, but I did all right without it."

Pruitt was piling up impressive numbers despite the Browns experiencing their worst era ever (up to that point). They were 4–10 in 1974 and 3–11 in 1975, only the second and third losing seasons ever for Cleveland. In 1976 the Browns rebounded to finish 9–5 and were in playoff contention all the way to the final weekend. The next fall, it looked as if the team was on its way when the bottom fell out in the second half of the season. The team finished in the AFC Central Division basement at 6–8.

"Pruitt was just a dynamic running back," said Mike Peticca. "He had elite quickness and flat-out speed. He could change direction without really losing a step. He had great vision. During a run, he could anticipate what the next challenge that he would face would be. He was the whole package. The big controversy was that Nick Skorich didn't utilize him more in '73 and '74. He had only four-and-a-half seasons with the Browns really where he was utilized to the extent that he should've been. He was a terrific receiver, too. He was just fun to watch."

"Greg was a great running back," Doug Dieken said. "He made that halfback option out of the backfield a bread-and-butter play for our offense. He was a bit of a finesse, fancy runner. Sometimes he'd use his quickness to set up a block."

"It was just stop-on-a-dime moves and of course his shirt tearing," McLain said. "Pound for pound, Pruitt was just a great player. He was just a ball of excitement."

"Being a Browns fan, especially in the '60s and '70s," Michael Cuomo said, "we were blessed with the greatest running back of all time, Jim Brown, and after him came Leroy Kelly, and after Kelly came Pruitt. We were just blessed with dynamic talent. When I would watch football, even to this day, you'll watch a running back and say, 'Well, he's a good runner, he's a power runner, but they have to take him out on third down because he can't catch the ball.' When I watched Brown, when I watched Kelly, when I watched Pruitt, you didn't have to take those guys out because they just caught the ball naturally. Greg Pruitt probably had the best hands on our team, and he was a running back. I challenge anybody to go back and watch films of him in games and how he was such a hands catcher. Late in his career, after he had that injury that robbed him a little bit of his running ability, he became more of a receiving back. The way he would just snatch the ball out of the air.... Pruitt was just dynamite. He was so much fun. Probably the only good thing Art Modell ever did was he allegedly said, 'We need to draft Greg Pruitt.'"

Pruitt also returned punts and kickoffs in his early years with the Browns. "I don't know if they make punt returners like that anymore," said McLain.

"What a punt returner he was," said Cuomo. "His feet were so quick."

As the Kardiac Kids were taking shape, Pruitt was dealt a major blow when he suffered a serious knee injury against the St. Louis Cardinals in Week 9 of 1979. He missed the rest of the season. The Browns, with the "other" Pruitt—fullback Mike Pruitt—barely missed the playoffs at 9–7, the seventh straight year the team failed to qualify. With Greg Pruitt back in 1980, now used mainly as a receiver out of the backfield, the Browns continued their thrill-a-minute ride and finally captured the AFC Central Division title, dethroning the two-time defending Super Bowl champion Steelers. He was on the receiving end of a clutch 21-yard pass from Brian Sipe on the final Browns drive of the "Red Right 88" loss to the Oakland Raiders that brought the 1980 season to a screeching halt. Pruitt's last season with the Browns was in 1981. He caught 65 passes that year, but the Browns plummeted to a 5–11 last-place finish. Pruitt was traded to the Oakland (soon-to-be Los Angeles) Raiders on April 28, 1982, where he spent three seasons mainly as a kick returner, duties he also assumed in his first three years in Cleveland. He was not exactly elated with the deal.

"I got so depressed, I contemplated retirement," he said.

After some encouragement from Browns running backs coach Jim Garrett, Pruitt decided the Browns were wrong about him and that he still had some gas left in the tank. He accepted the move that sent him out west. Pruitt will never forget when he and defensive end Lyle Alzado, traded from the Browns to the Raiders the same day Pruitt was, first walked into the Raiders' training camp that summer.

"They introduced all the veterans from all the other teams first," Pruitt recalled. "And they introduced us last. They all clapped and gave us a standing ovation. Lyle said, 'They must think we can still play!' They heard him and said, 'No, no, no … because of you guys, we've got these,' and they started holding their [Super Bowl] rings up."

The Raiders' players were referring to the "Red Right 88" play two seasons before that helped propel them to the Super Bowl XV title. Along with Alzado, Pruitt exacted a little revenge on his old team that had traded him as he helped Los Angeles to a playoff win over Cleveland his first season there, and even earned a Super Bowl ring of his own the next season when the Raiders won Super Bowl XVIII over the Washington Redskins.

Pruitt's finest rushing performance came against the Chiefs on December 14, 1975, when he gained 214 yards on 26 carries in a 40–14 Browns rout. Other great rushing performances included a 191-yard display against the Falcons in 1976 and a 182-yarder in 1978 against the Bengals. Pruitt rushed for 5,496 yards and 25 touchdowns with the Browns. His longest run was a 78-yarder for a score against Kansas City in 1977. In addition, he caught 323 passes for 3,022 yards and 17 touchdowns as a Brown. Pruitt, once a quarterback in high school, even passed for six touchdowns with Cleveland, the longest a 60-yarder to Gloster Richardson against Cincinnati in 1974. He also returned a kickoff 88 yards for a score against the Patriots that same year. Pruitt was a Pro Bowler in 1973, 1974, 1976, and 1977.

In 1979 Pruitt won ABC's *Superstars*, an all-around sports competition that pitted elite athletes from different sports against one another in a series of athletic events resembling a decathlon. How he got on the show was rather interesting. Pruitt watched previous *Superstars* competitions and felt he could do better than the athletes he saw on the shows. Pruitt asked his agent to get him on the show, and his agent called ABC. All the athletes on *Superstars* were picked by the network to be on the show, so Pruitt wrote a letter to the network explaining why he should be on the show.

"That's how he got on the show!" Coughlin said. "He asked a couple of other NFL players who were on the show in the past what they wrote in their letters to get on the show. They didn't know what the hell he was talking about. They said, 'You wrote a letter?' So Pruitt became the butt of jokes because he wrote a letter to get on the show when everyone else was picked by the network to be on the show.

"And he won the damn thing!"

Pruitt, who is 73 years old and runs his own contracting business called Pruitt and Associates, had high marks for the Cleveland faithful.

"Those fans are better than anybody," he said.

Jerry Sherk probably said it best when describing Pruitt's talents as a running back.

"There were a few times where we, as a team, watched the game films together," he said. "Even watching the game films, my teammates and myself would get so excited from watching Greg run that we would just start yelling. He would do things that were just so unbelievable. He had breakaway speed. He was really one of the most exciting, dynamic, and prolific runners of that era."

Greg Pruitt trying to elude Pittsburgh's
Jack Lambert (58) and Mean Joe Greene, 1975
Malcolm W. Emmons/Wikimedia Commons

9

THE THREE RIVERS JINX

Jinx, as defined by Dictionary.com: "A person, thing, or influence supposed to bring bad luck."

Jinx, as could have been defined by the Browns of the 1970s and early to mid-1980s: "A thing, namely Three Rivers Stadium, supposed to bring bad luck."

Beginning with a 28–9 defeat on November 29, 1970, the Browns lost 16 consecutive games at Three Rivers, the home of their archrivals, the Pittsburgh Steelers, who moved into the brand-new stadium that very same year of 1970. The Steelers spent their previous 37 seasons in Pitt Stadium on the University of Pittsburgh campus and at Forbes Field.

Not coincidentally, the start of the losing streak coincided with the arrival of one Terry Bradshaw in "Steel Town." The young quarterback was Pittsburgh's top pick—and the number one overall selection—in the 1970 NFL draft, held in January of that year. Although Three Rivers Stadium itself was believed by many Browns fans to be "haunted," Bradshaw, the ex-Louisiana Tech University star with a rifle of a right arm, had much to do with the Steelers' dominance of the Browns in

Pittsburgh, which eventually came to be known as the "Three Rivers Jinx."

The fact that Pittsburgh was one of the NFL's best teams during much of the streak's duration should make its success against Cleveland at home come as no surprise. However, at the same time they found the going rough in southwestern Pennsylvania, the Browns were able to muster road wins over other top teams, including Miami in 1970, Oakland in 1973, and both Cincinnati and San Francisco in 1981 (the latter season in which the Browns had a losing record). One would think that once—just once—Cleveland would have pulled one out in Pittsburgh, stolen one, somewhere along the way.

Pittsburgh's mastery of the Browns at home during this period came during a time when Cleveland was on the downswing and Pittsburgh the upswing. Heading into the 1970 season—the year of the NFL-AFL merger—the Browns had a rich tradition, having won four NFL championships (appearing in 11 title games) in their 20 years in the league; they won eight championships in all including four in the All-America Football Conference. They had treated Pittsburgh like a whipping bag for years, winning 31 of 40 games including 15 of 20 on the road. The Steelers, on the other hand, had never won a title of any kind in their nearly 40-year history except for perhaps that of ... well ... loser.

"The Steelers were turnpike rivals to the Browns the first 20 years of the rivalry, but they weren't really rivals in the sense that Pittsburgh hardly won," said Steve King. "The Browns' real rivals from that time were the Giants and, toward the end of the '60s, the St. Louis Cardinals and the Dallas Cowboys. It never really was Pittsburgh other than just a proximity rivalry.

"With that having been said, when Pittsburgh built that new stadium in 1970 and the Browns went over there, there was no fear of playing in that stadium or no fear of playing in Pittsburgh. Even when the Browns lost their first couple games over there by decided margins, it was just, 'Okay, whatever.' You didn't really think about it. It was just, 'Maybe they caught 'em on a good day.'"

After an easy win over the Browns in Three Rivers in 1971, Pittsburgh's home victory over Cleveland in 1972 was notable not for its competitiveness but for another reason: the marking of the changing of the guard. The Browns were an aging team attempting to make one last stand. The Steelers were in the midst of building a dynasty. Former Browns linebacker/guard Chuck Noll was in his fourth year as Pittsburgh's head coach, and through excellent drafting, had improved his team drastically from a 1–13 record in his first season to an 8–3 mark entering this December 3 contest against the Browns, who were also 8–3 and had beaten the same Steelers just two weeks earlier.

In this battle for AFC Central Division supremacy, the battle turned into a Three Rivers thrashing as Pittsburgh routed the Browns, 30–0, holding them to a measly 126 total yards. The Browns finished second at 10–4 but still qualified for the playoffs as the AFC wild card team. It would turn out to be the proud franchise's last postseason appearance until the dawning of the next decade. Both the Steelers and Browns were ousted by eventual Super Bowl champion Miami, the Browns in the divisional round and the Steelers in the conference championship game.

"It wasn't until that 1972 game," said King, "when you started thinking, 'Hey, this is something real, maybe something has changed over there, maybe they have better players, this might not be the same old Steelers.' That '72 game was kind of the exclamation point behind it. You have to remember, Noll's first three Steelers teams were 1–13, 5–9, and 6–8. It wasn't this complete metamorphosis, everything changing in one fell swoop. They had the good sense to do what they do now over there, and that is let a coach develop. So those teams got better incrementally, and then all of a sudden in '72 it kind of blossomed. That 30–0 game in '72 was a physical beating as well as a beating on the scoreboard. That was the game that flipped the rivalry. It wasn't for two or three more years until the Steelers started winning some in Cleveland because they hadn't won in Cleveland since 1964. The Steelers would win in Pittsburgh starting in the '70s, but they'd still lose in Cleveland. So that '72 game was the first nail in the coffin, but when the

Steelers went to Cleveland and won in 1974, all of a sudden it's like, 'Hey, this thing is starting to flip.'"

With the tide now turned, the Steelers won the next four home games against the Browns, three of them with at least relative ease.

Beginning in 1977, the heart of the Jinx took its course, as the next five games in Three Rivers between the "turnpike rivals" hinged on hard hits and thrilling finishes, not to mention some suspect officiating. In the five games from 1977 to 1981, Pittsburgh won by an average of just 4.4 points per game. The following is a recap of the Browns-Steelers games at Three Rivers Stadium from 1977 to 1981:

- Pittsburgh 35, Browns 31
  (November 13, 1977)

   Quarterback Brian Sipe fractures his left shoulder blade and misses the rest of the season. Backup Dave Mays leads a furious fourth-quarter rally that falls just short.

- Pittsburgh 15, Browns 9 (OT)
  (September 24, 1978)

   In an early-season showdown for first place, Ricky Feacher recovers a fumble by return man Larry Anderson on the overtime kickoff deep in Steelers territory. Although television replays —and the NFL the next day—confirm that Anderson was not touched by a single Brown when he falls to the ground before getting up, running, and fumbling the ball, officials rule that the Steelers' rookie was down by contact, and the ball is awarded to Pittsburgh. Moments later, Bradshaw hits tight end Bennie Cunningham for a 37-yard touchdown pass on a flea flicker. According to Sam Rutigliano, the Browns' head coach at the time, team owner Art Modell was so enraged that he would be fined $25,000 by the NFL due to his incessant banging on the door to the officials dressing room after the game.

- Pittsburgh 33, Browns 30 (OT)
  (November 25, 1979)

  Cleveland enters 8–4, just a game behind Pittsburgh and a game-and-a-half behind Houston. The Browns squander leads of 20–6, 27–13, and 30–20. They trail one time—when future Brown Matt Bahr connects on a 37-yard field goal with nine seconds left in sudden death.

- Pittsburgh 16, Browns 13
  (November 16, 1980)

  Bradshaw's three-yard touchdown pass to wide receiver Lynn Swann with 11 seconds to go—a play in which Steelers wideout Theo Bell admits after the game that he illegally picked Browns cornerback Ron Bolton—gives Pittsburgh the victory and costs the Browns a share of first place.

- Pittsburgh 13, Browns 7
  (October 11, 1981)

    Paul McDonald replaces a dazed Sipe, who suffers a concussion from a ferocious hit by linebacker Jack Lambert in the third quarter. McDonald leads his team on two late drives, but an interception on a tipped pass in the Steelers' end zone kills one; time expires on the other when officials rule that receiver Reggie Rucker fails to get out of bounds—Rucker claims he did—after his 17-yard reception moves Cleveland to the Pittsburgh 32 yard line.

"Every year it was something different," said Michael Cuomo. "One year they were just too good for the Browns, another year the Browns would outplay them but the refs would totally screw them, and other years the ball wouldn't bounce the Browns' way. They always gave it a good effort."

The Browns' frustration at their failings in Three Rivers Stadium led them to the depths of superstition. Chuck Heaton, the team's beat writer for the *Cleveland Plain Dealer* from 1954 to 1977 and who covered the club part-time for several years thereafter, recalled the

Browns resorting to extreme measures in trying to halt the Jinx.

"They tried flying to Pittsburgh, they took a bus for a while … I think one time they even drove over in cars," he said. "They also changed hotels several times."

"Sometimes I wondered if we were going to ask for volunteers to go to Pittsburgh," joked Rutigliano, Cleveland's head coach from 1978 until midway through the 1984 season, in his autobiography *Pressure*.

In all sincerity, though, Rutigliano did not buy into the whole "Jinx" phenomenon, and neither did his assistant coaches or his players. "The Steelers were just a great team," he said. "Before the 1978 game we were undefeated, and they were undefeated, and we got screwed on the first play of overtime and lost the game. So I took the moment and said to the players in the locker room, 'Look, let's capture THE MOMENT. Now, listen to me because I'm only gonna talk for about two or three minutes. This is the best team in the world! And I want you to know that there are gonna be 10 or 12 [players on that Steelers team] who are gonna be enshrined in Canton, Ohio, about 25 years from now. Let's be able to understand what you did against this kind of a team."

"They had a pretty good defense over there," said Doug Dieken, winning the Understatement of the Year Award. "So they were a pretty complete football team. Of the 11 guys they had on the defense, I think at some point or another 10 of them went to the Pro Bowl, four of them are in the Hall of Fame, and there's a fifth one that's trying to get in. So that was a pretty talented football team."

"Let's face it," Mike McLain said, "the Steelers back in the 1970s when they were on were unbeatable. Their defense was … you couldn't get a first down let alone a touchdown against them. They were just a special team that came together. And in the '70s the Browns weren't very good. There's no jinx there when you're getting punched in the mouth all the time."

"I think the only way it could have been a jinx is that players are human, and maybe it filters down to them," Mike Peticca said. "When they have a lead in '79, say, Bradshaw might complete some to Swann or Stallworth as they're trying to come back. Players are human— maybe from the standpoint of a 'Here we go again' type thing. The Steelers were simply better, though."

"There may have been a little bit of a jinx in terms of us players thinking we could just not win in Three Rivers, but I think the majority of it was that the Steelers were a better team," Jerry Sherk said. "I can remember going into Three Rivers once or twice and playing them really close in the first half, staying within three or seven points. You could just tell that the Steelers didn't have the hammer down, that they had kind of a lackadaisical attitude, and were kind of smiling and joking. Then they come out of halftime, and it was like a different team. Maybe Chuck Noll had chewed them out. In the third quarter they'd score three touchdowns, and the game's pretty much over. As a player, it's kind of like operant conditioning. Every time you see Three Rivers Stadium and that terrible, hard AstroTurf, it's kind of like, 'Well, here we go again. We're in this place in which we always walk out a beat-up dog.'"

The Browns' defensive backfield, namely the safeties, did its part in trying to halt the Jinx. "We said, 'Look, we're going to try to deliver some blows to these guys so they realize that they're not going to be wide open and maybe think about focusing their attention on getting hit rather than the ball," said Thom Darden. "Back then, our thought was always if you knock somebody out, you would be better served because they would be thinking about where the hit is coming from rather than focusing their attention solely on catching the ball.

"Our offensive line, I think, though, felt a little bit intimidated by the 'Steel Curtain,' but by no stretch of the imagination were we intimidated as a team by the Steelers. We felt we were just as good as, right there with, them. They just seemed to be able to keep our offense from scoring and score on our defense at the necessary times, especially going down the stretch. They were close games, and they were good games. They were always hard, tough-fought games."

Like his coach, Darden did not believe the Browns were jinxed.

"I just considered it solely a black eye on our team," he said.

"Soon after I got to Cleveland," Ozzie Newsome, a Browns tight end from 1978 to 1990, said, "the sheer hatred that the Browns and their fans have for the Pittsburgh Steelers became apparent ... people would talk to me and would be like, 'Oh, you're the draft choice ... ya'll gonna beat Pittsburgh this year?' So you start to realize that, and they were comparing the rivalry to me: 'Well, it's bigger than your Alabama-Auburn rivalry.' And I go, 'What? Bigger than Alabama-Auburn?' And they say, 'Yes. It is.' You live Alabama-Auburn every day because your next-door neighbor could be an Auburn graduate. But the week of the game, the Cleveland-Pittsburgh rivalry is more so. So, right away, you realize the importance of it, but, at that time, Pittsburgh ... they had already won two Super Bowls, and you just start to think about the players who they had playing. So, again, this is me being on the field with a bunch of future Hall of Famers who I grew up idolizing ... Stallworth, Swann and Franco and Joe Greene and Mel Blount, and now I'm on the same field with those guys."

After lopsided losses in Three Rivers in 1982 and 1983, the Browns were defeated on last-second field goals the next two years, but the tide was slowly turning back in favor of Cleveland. By the time the 1986 season began, the Browns' talent level was far superior to the Steelers' for the first time since the streak began, and the

"Three Rivers Jinx" finally came to an end on October 5 of that year. Cleveland defeated Pittsburgh, 27–24, that day—highlighted by Gerald "The Ice Cube" McNeil's 100-yard kickoff return for a touchdown—the first of four straight wins for the Browns in what will forever be known as their own personal "House of Horrors."

"I can remember, in retirement in California," Sherk recalled, "I was driving somewhere on a Sunday, and I somehow had the 1986 Browns-at-Steelers game on the radio, and it looked like the Browns were going to win with Bernie Kosar at Three Rivers. I pulled over to the side of road and listened. And when that final gun went off I went, '*Finally*, the Browns have beaten Pittsburgh in Pittsburgh.'"

Dieken, ever the comedian, concluded, "The first game of the streak was the year before I was drafted by the Browns, and the last game of the streak was the year after I retired.

"So you can't blame it on me."

Three Rivers Stadium
Escapedtowisconsin/Wikimedia Commons

10

DOUG DIEKEN:
FROM PLAYER TO BROADCASTER

Nineteen-eighty was certainly not Doug Dieken's finest season. Far from it. Funny thing is, it was his only Pro Bowl year.

"It kind of shows how the voting goes," the former Browns offensive left tackle explained. "If you win, you've got a better chance of going to the Pro Bowl than if you lose. I mean, I played the season on kind of one leg. I had strained knee ligaments. By far, it wasn't the best season I ever had."

Joining Dieken in Honolulu were four of his teammates, including fellow offensive linemen Joe DeLamielleure and Tom DeLeone, making for the "Three Ds."

Hailing from the small town of Streator, Illinois, some 100 miles southwest of Chicago, Dieken had been to just one professional football game before joining the Browns. Ironically, it was a Browns game—against the Bears on November 30, 1969, at Wrigley Field. A sixth-round draft pick of the Browns in 1971 out of the University of Illinois, where he majored in education,

Dieken joined a Cleveland team stocked with veterans accustomed to championship-level football, several of them still around from the team's last NFL title in 1964. A wide receiver and tight end in college, Dieken made the team and by November of his rookie season had bulked up and taken over for longtime left tackle Dick Schafrath. Dieken carried on the franchise's fine tradition at the position, at one time manned by Lou "The Toe" Groza.

"When they switched Doug from tight end to tackle," Jerry Sherk recalled, "I can remember some early practices where he hardly knew how to line up or how to get into his stance. He developed so rapidly, though, it was just unbelievable. Within a couple months, he was a pretty solid offensive tackle, and then he went on to have a great career. He had a really strong upper body, really strong arms, and he was known for his ability to hold legally. The time where holding legally comes in handy is in pass protection. He could hold legally better than anybody I knew on pass protection. If you hold within the confines of the shoulder pad, if you can grab a guy sort of right at the breast area and keep him in front of you because of your grip and your footwork, the refs won't call it. Anytime you get out of those confines, you'll get called for it. He was so proud of that."

"Dieken looked to be a very good player right away," Mike Peticca said. "It became kind of a joke, the holding thing, people joking about him being called for holding all the time. I thought he was a good player right at the start. I just remember so much his determination and his pride. I think he had an attitude that carried over to the rest of the team, most specifically the offensive line. It was of great benefit to the whole team. He was really smart. I know all the players looked up to him. I think it took great guys on the other side of the ball to sometimes, and only occasionally, get the best of him. I think his good humor diminished the perspective on him that his humor and attitude kind of overshadowed how really good he was."

Early in his career, Dieken pulled double duty as he also played on the special teams. "I don't think there are many starting offensive tackles that do that crap anymore," he said. "We had an older team. We had the remnants of the '64 championship team. You had Schafrath, you had Gene Hickerson, you had Jim Houston, you had Erich Barnes. You had a lot of older guys ... *they* weren't going to be playing on special teams anymore. That's just the way the game was back then. You only had like 37 guys on the team back then. You didn't have this expanded roster like they have now."

Although the Browns, for the most part, were average at best during his playing days, Dieken nonetheless was involved in a number of memorable games. Long before the Kardiac Kids era, there was the AFC divisional playoff on Christmas Eve 1972 in the Orange Bowl when the Browns had the undefeated Dolphins on the ropes in the fourth quarter. Five interceptions by Mike Phipps, however, doomed the Browns during a 20–14 defeat.

The mid-1970s brought consecutive losing seasons for the first time in franchise history—4–10 in 1974, Nick Skorich's final season as head coach, and 3–11 in 1975, Forrest Gregg's first.

"It was frustrating," acknowledged Dieken, explaining that age, retirements, and poor drafting were the main reasons for the decline. The Browns improved to an extent under Gregg but really got it in gear when Sam Rutigliano came aboard and Brian Sipe began blossoming into a top-flight quarterback in 1978. Then came the Kardiac Kids experience in 1979 and 1980 when the Browns took their fans on a wild ride of thrilling finishes.

Perhaps Dieken's most gratifying individual memory occurred on October 30, 1983, in a home game against the Houston Oilers. His receiving skills from college came in handy when he caught a 14-yard touchdown pass from Paul McDonald on a fake field goal, the lone touchdown of his professional career. Dieken said the play was actually designed to go to kicker Matt Bahr to pick up a first down. "But when I came off the line of scrimmage, everybody was up on the line rushing," he recalled, "and I was so wide open that McDonald couldn't miss me."

Dieken's final season was in 1984. It was one to forget. The Browns were competitive in almost every game, they just fell apart in the fourth quarter. They finished 5–11. "I was going to try to come back for another year," Dieken said, "but Marty Schottenheimer [who had replaced Rutigliano at the midway point of 1984] decided since they were going to get a new quarterback, they might as well get a new left tackle, so ... we decided to call it quits. I was fortunate enough to hang around for 14 years and figured I got my money's worth out of my body."

"Dieken was so reliable," said Michael Cuomo. "I know he always jokes that he made a career out of holding, but believe me, if he held that much, he never would've been a stud tackle in the league for 14 years. He was damn good; he was damn good. I think he learned from Schafrath that whenever a Brown scored a touchdown, he'd run to the end zone and shake their hand."

"People forget what a solid left tackle he was. He was an underrated player," Mike McLain said. "You think of Dick Schafrath and Joe Thomas ... sometimes people forget that old number 73 was in there. I consider him 'Mr. Cleveland Brown' because he was involved with that team as long as he was."

"He really understood the game and knew how to play the position," Steve King said. "He knew positioning, footwork, all of that."

Added Fred Hoaglin, "Doug was a really good player and a real good competitor."

Dieken's retirement was timely—at least in a career

sense. It coincided with longtime Browns radio voice Gib Shanley's exodus to "bigger and better" things in California. Dieken and newcomer Nev Chandler joined Jim Mueller in the booth. Dieken was a fixture there until he retired following the 2021 season. Right off the bat, he got to call the action during some high times for the Browns, including the painful divisional playoff loss to the Dolphins in 1985, the amazing, double-overtime comeback playoff win over the Jets in 1986 and, of course, the infamous "Drive" and "Fumble" defeats, the first two of the three-part "Denver Dilemma." Does Dieken believe the Browns would have won any of the three Super Bowls had they beaten the Broncos in any of those AFC Championship games?

"I think once you get there, you just kind of roll the dice. I think there's a chance they would've [won at least one]," he said, adding that, even had the Browns advanced to—and won— one of those Super Bowls, he believes the franchise still would have wound up in Baltimore. "I think the game got to be too much of a rich man's game for [Art] Modell to afford the team. I mean, he was in financial trouble whether they won or not. His problem was he wasn't the best businessman. He made some financial decisions that came back to haunt him. And it gets to the point where you've got to have money to play the game, and he didn't have that kind of money there everybody else had."

Dieken, who also had several local gigs as a sports

reporter after his playing days, including positions at WEWS TV-5 and WKYC TV-3, not only had the misfortune of taking part in the infamous NFL players' strike of 1982, he was a central figure in a "work" stoppage as a senior at Illinois.

"They fired our coach [Jim Valek] in the middle of the season, right after the Ohio State game, and we actually played Ohio State pretty good," Dieken remembered. "We had them down at half but lost by [more than] a couple touchdowns. [Ohio State head coach] Woody Hayes said if they fired [Valek] for being a bad coach, they [Ohio State] should fire [Hayes] because [Valek] outcoached him that day."

A private team meeting was held in the locker room. Dieken stood up and told his teammates that if Valek was gone, he was too.

"Everybody said that they were going to join me, so we took the University of Illinois football team out on strike," he said. "The athletic department had an emergency meeting, and they hired [Valek] for the remainder of the season. And then the next week, we went over to Purdue for their homecoming and beat them and gave the coach the game ball."

The 75-year-old Dieken, who resides in the Cleveland area, is partners with former Browns teammate and fellow offensive lineman Robert E. Jackson in ownership of a local insurance company. He has a grown son and daughter and three grandchildren.

Dieken has fond memories of his playing days and was thrilled that he had the good fortune of staying associated with the Browns via the airwaves. Perfect timing, he said, was critical in both cases. "I happened to be coming to the Browns when Dick Schafrath was getting a little old," he said, "and then I retired, and when Gib Shanley decided to go out to the West Coast and be a sportscaster out there, that opened up a job here.

"So, between the two of them, I just happened to be in the right place at the right time."

Doug Dieken, March 18, 1976
Martin Brown/Wikimedia Commons

11

THE MIKE PHIPPS EXPERIMENT

When the Browns traded wide receiver Paul Warfield to the Miami Dolphins on January 26, 1970, in exchange for the third pick in the following day's NFL draft, it was Ron Harper for Danny Ferry two decades early.

The Browns coveted sensational quarterback Mike Phipps from Purdue University—and got him. Phipps had led the Boilermakers to 24 wins in 30 games – including a pair of Associated Press top 10 rankings—the three previous autumns. The move sent shock waves throughout the city of Cleveland reminiscent of when the Cleveland Cavaliers shipped Harper, the spectacular shooting guard, along with three draft picks, to the Los Angeles Clippers for forward Danny "I ain't quite Larry) Ferry and guard Reggie Williams in November 1989.

The Warfield trade caused confusion and heartache among several Browns players. One was Jim Houston, a Browns linebacker from 1960 to 1972. "It didn't make sense to me. I don't know what went on in the background or up in the offices," Houston said in the NFL Films documentary *The Cleveland Browns: Fifty Years of Memories.*

Billy Andrews believed the move likely cost the Browns a chance to be in the Super Bowl that year. "The 1970 team, I thought, was one of the better teams that I had played on," Andrews said in the same documentary.

Phipps played sparingly in 1970 and 1971 while backing up veteran Bill Nelsen, whose bad knees were the main reason the Browns drafted Phipps. Phipps became the full-time starter one game into the 1972 season. That '72 campaign would be his best as a Brown as he led Cleveland to the playoffs and a near upset of the Warfield-led, undefeated Dolphins in the divisional round. But Phipps that year passed for just 1,994 yards with 13 touchdown passes against 16 interceptions. While Warfield was busy winning Super Bowls in the Sunshine State, Phipps was on his way to some mighty struggles in Cleveland, the low point coming in 1974 and 1975 when he combined for 13 touchdown passes and 36 interceptions as the Browns won just seven of 28 games. His touchdowns-to-interceptions ratios from 1973 to 1975 were 9 TDs/20 INTs in 1973, 9/17 in 1974, and 4/19 in 1975.

"Mike was a physical specimen. That guy was built," Thom Darden said. "Obviously, he had a strong arm, but I don't think he was mentally as tough as Brian Sipe. To me, that's the biggest difference in the National Football League. All the guys who come in there are physically capable. It's how your mindset, your mentality, takes over. Are you going to hang your head when things don't go right and hide? Are you going to run away from guys who are bigger and stronger than you? It takes some inner strength to not do that. I think Mike kind of curled up a little bit sometimes. He had a lot of talent. He was smart, he was a smart guy. There is a disconnect sometimes, though, between your mental capability and your football mental capability, and if those two things are not in line you could be the best physical specimen there is, but if you don't have the mental strength, the mental stick-to-itiveness, you're not going to be successful on that field."

"Mike had the same talent that Terry Bradshaw had. He had all of the tools that Bradshaw had," Andrews said. "But, in my little knowledge that I have of football is that Mike had tunnel vision, and he couldn't see anybody but the one player who he had chosen to throw to. He had the brains, the physical talent, everything necessary."

"I thought we made a huge mistake," said Fred Hoaglin. "Paul Warfield was such a great player, and you don't trade players like that. In order to stop him or just limit him, they had to double team him, and teams couldn't even do *that*. Nobody could cover him man-for-man. When you have a weapon like that, you don't trade him because he can do something that nobody else can do. Plus, to take his place we got Homer Jones, who still had great speed but wasn't Paul Warfield."

Hoaglin remembers the moment Phipps was inserted at quarterback with the first-string offense to relieve

Nelsen during the Browns' exhibition game against the Cincinnati Bengals in 1970.

"Phipps came in the huddle and said, 'Okay, guys, give me some help. I'm gonna try and move the ball,'" Hoaglin said. "And I'm thinking under my breath—and maybe everybody else was, too—'Okay, we just went down the field twice and scored touchdowns, so we can *do* that. You just do *your* job.' I thought, 'That's not quite the way to lead a football team.'"

Doug Dieken feels Phipps simply did not have a passion for the game of football. "He was a good, natural athlete, and things had come easily for him before he got to the pros," he said. "But he just wasn't able to elevate it in the pros."

"Mike had tremendous talent," Jerry Sherk said, "but sometimes it just felt like he didn't have a complete feel for the game."

Blanton Collier was the Browns' head coach when the team drafted Phipps. According to Dan Coughlin, Collier was adamantly against trading Warfield for the right to draft Phipps.

"Blanton and I were planning on doing his life story in a book, but then he caught cancer and died, so we never got it done," Coughlin said. "But he and I would sit for long periods of time around his kitchen table near Houston. One night we started talking about some issues with Phipps. He said he was not in favor of the trade because of, most of all, losing Paul Warfield. He said

Warfield not only was a great receiver but he always made the key block on the power sweep, that he never missed a block. His block was on the cornerback, and he never missed it. With Warfield gone, the power sweep slowed to a crawl. They didn't have another wide receiver who could make that block. I can remember Blanton telling me that he was in a meeting with Art Modell and his advisors and that he was the only one in the room who voted against trading Warfield to get that draft pick. Getting ready for the draft, they knew they were going to pick Phipps. Blanton talked to some of his contacts at Purdue, and he did not get great reports on Phipps's acumen. They said he didn't have a great mind for football. Did he have a great dedication to improve his mind for football? No.

"After the draft, Blanton tries to tutor Phipps, and he would meet with him regularly whether in Cleveland or at Purdue. He'd sit with him and he gave him a notebook and he said, 'Make notes of what I'm telling you.' They would talk and talk and talk … and then Blanton noticed Phipps never wrote down a thing. Blanton said, 'I'm sure I must've said something that was worth remembering. Never wrote down a thing.' And that's how it went. Phipps came to Cleveland, Blanton continued to try to tutor him, but it was falling on deaf ears. He didn't write down a thing. That was Blanton's view of what happened with the Phipps deal. It took the Browns a long time to recover from that trade."

"When I covered Browns in 1980, we used to sit in Sam Rutigliano's office after practice, me and Russ Schneider, Ray Yannucci, and a bunch of us," Mike McLain recalled. "We'd just shoot the breeze. One time, we were talking about Mike Phipps and someone said, 'If a squirrel ran up his leg, there wouldn't be anything to munch on,' basically saying he didn't have any balls. Comparing Phipps to Brian Sipe, obviously Phipps had so much more natural ability, but I just think he didn't have the moxie that Sipe had for a few years. As far as I'm concerned, from what I understand from those in the know, Phipps just didn't have the moxie."

On the other side of the argument, there are those who believe Phipps's poor career in Cleveland had a lot to do with the talent surrounding him. Mike Peticca is one of those people.

"From the second game of the 1972 season when Phipps took over for Nelsen as the starter to the 12th game of the 1973 season, the Browns were 17–6–2," said Peticca. "When Phipps took over, both Gary Collins and Paul Warfield were gone, and he had probably a below-average receiving core. Phipps was excellent at scrambling, but from what I heard, they discouraged him from running. They wanted him to stay in the pocket. If that's so, that they discouraged him from getting out of the pocket and running the ball, that took away from any edge he had. That's all relevant to the dilemma he was facing because, like I said, he had maybe a less-than-average receiving core. Frank Pitts was pretty good, but when Frank Pitts is your best guy, that's not great. Milt Morin was still pretty good but approaching a little beyond his prime years. Also, Dick Schafrath had retired at the end of '71, and Gene Hickerson was still good, but he was past his prime. They didn't have a great offensive line. Leroy Kelly was no longer the running back he had been, had been worn down from a series of not debilitating, but nagging, leg and ankle injuries. Phipps just didn't have much around him. To me, he was a combination of circumstances that did not allow him to really demonstrate the abilities he probably had."

"Phipps had a great arm, there was no question about it, he had a fantastic arm," said Steve King. "I don't think that he was a leader, but more so than anything else I think it was just the timing of it. That team got old around him. All those players from the '60s and even a couple back into the '50s all got old at the same time. You see that with great teams. They have a cluster of players, and when those guys get old all at the same time it's a problem. Drafting near the bottom for all those years caught up with them. Mistakes on personnel caught up with them. So I think Phipps was the byproduct in a lot of ways of poor players around him and a bad offensive line that had deteriorated. He wasn't the quarterback they thought he was, but at the same time that team around him was not good from the end of the 1973 season on. They were tied for first place with two games left in '73, lost the last two games, and that carried over into '74 and '75. Reggie Rucker always told me that the hardest, best ball that he got from any of the Browns quarterbacks, including Brian Sipe, was from Mike Phipps. He had ability. When you draft a guy number three, the pressure is all on him. Terry Bradshaw was in that draft. He didn't work out right away because they had a bad team around him. You have to have the quarterback, no question about it, but you have to have some players around him."

"Before I got there," Rucker said, "they had no receivers for him to throw to. They had nothing. Phipps had everything—the size, the arm, he could run, he could do it all. He just didn't have any receivers."

Admitted Thom Darden, "Mike might've been gun shy because when he went back to pass, he got hit most of the time."

Michael Cuomo said it remains a mystery as to why Phipps did not make it in Cleveland, but he has some theories. "Obviously, we had Bill Nelsen," he said. "Back then, it was quite normal for a quarterback—I don't care if he was the first pick in the draft—to have to wait his turn and to learn by observing. That was the normal path to becoming a quarterback. I mean, it wasn't even unusual if a quarterback sat for three, four, five years before he became a starter. Mike Phipps was an enigma as to why he didn't make it. He had all the tools. When he came out of Purdue, he was a more polished product than Terry Bradshaw was, who was a raw product who was drafted ahead of him out of Louisiana Tech. It's just a mystery that Phipps didn't make it. Back then, it was a different world. The game wasn't covered to the level it is now, so he wasn't dissected. But I can tell you this. He was 6-foot-3, 208 pounds, a big quarterback by even today's standards, some 50 years later. He was mobile as all get out. He could run, he could escape. Everybody remembers the play he made against the Steelers—it was the mud game in 1973—where he scrambled around and eluded one Steeler in the backfield and then threw a pass to Greg Pruitt about 30 yards downfield, and then Pruitt took it down to about the 20 yard line. It's one of the greatest football plays you'll ever see. Did he not comprehend coverages? Was that his Achilles heel? Could've been. I've heard murmurings that he was just too quiet and wasn't a leader type. I don't know if that's true. I have no idea. But that doesn't make sense to me because, when he was at Purdue, he was a big-time leader, so I don't understand why eventually that wouldn't translate to the pros. Now that I'm almost 70 years old, I understand that character, leadership, intangibles do matter. I could see how, if you're lacking completely in that, or maybe you're just not a confident person … just because somebody is a good athlete doesn't mean they're naturally confident. Something was amiss. Like I said, it's a mystery, and to this day I don't get it."

Phipps did have his moments, and his finest may have come in Cleveland's home game against Cincinnati on November 23, 1975. The Bengals entered with a sparkling 8–1 record and were tied atop the AFC Central Division with Pittsburgh. The Browns, meanwhile, were at their lowest point in their fabled 30-year history at the time. They were 0–9 in Forrest Gregg's first season as head coach. Seven defeats had come by double-digit margins. Down by eight points in the fourth quarter in front of 56,427 fans, the Browns exploded, scoring more points—20—in one quarter than they had scored in one game all year. Phipps completed a five-yard touchdown pass to Oscar Roan on which the tight end made a circus catch to cut the Bengals' lead to one. Phipps then hit Greg Pruitt for a 13-yard touchdown strike as the Browns forged ahead, 29–23. On that same drive, Phipps had connected with Pruitt for a 48-yard catch-and-run. The Browns went on to win, 35–23. Phipps had his finest day as a pro, completing 23 of 36 passes for 298 yards, the first time he ever eclipsed the 200-yard plateau. An even bigger surprise was that Phipps, who threw more than two interceptions for every touchdown pass (81 to 40) in his seven years with the Browns, did not throw a single pick all day long.

"Finally, by 1976," said Peticca, "Warfield was back. He wasn't himself, but he still knew what he was doing, he still had to pay attention. They had Reggie Rucker, and Dave Logan was a rookie. The offensive line had improved somewhat. And he had Mike Pruitt and Greg Pruitt. So you finally have a representative offense around Phipps, and he had a good training camp and a good exhibition season."

Phipps remained the starter when the '76 season opened on September 12 against the New York Jets in Cleveland. Phipps turned in another of his rare fine performances the Browns expected of him on a regular basis when they drafted him. With the Browns trailing, 10–0, in the second quarter, he brought the crowd of 67,496 to life by firing three touchdown passes—two to Rucker and one to Warfield— to give his team a 21–10 halftime lead. Alas, Phipps's shining moment ended early in the third quarter when Shafer Suggs fell on him making a tackle on a bootleg down the right sideline. Phipps suffered a separated right shoulder that knocked him out of the game and opened the door for Sipe, who took over and carried the torch in finishing off the Jets, 38–17.

In hindsight, the injury to Phipps, who was traded to the Bears in the offseason, was a blessing in disguise for the Browns, considering the magic wand Sipe would wave over the North Coast in the years to come.

Mike Phipps, 1975
Malcolm W. Emmons/Wikimedia Commons

12

TURKEY JONES TURNS TERRY BRADSHAW INTO A PRETZEL

Despite his team's 1–3 record to start the 1976 season, Terry Bradshaw likely did not expect his Pittsburgh Steelers to drop to 1–4 with a loss to the lowly Browns, also 1–3, on October 10 in Cleveland. Bradshaw certainly did not expect to be turned into a pretzel by Cleveland defensive end Joe "Turkey" Jones.

It wasn't much of a surprise that the Browns entered the game at 1–3, but it was a shocker that the Steelers did. The Browns were coming off two seasons that produced just seven wins combined. The Steelers were coming off two seasons that produced a pair of Super Bowl championships. The last time Cleveland beat Pittsburgh was in 1973. They had lost five in a row to the Steelers. The Steelers' lone victory of the 1976 season had come in week two against none other than the Browns. The loser of their Week 5 game would be in deep trouble, for AFC Central rivals Cincinnati and Houston were both 3–1.

In front of 76,411 fans, each team scored twice in the first half, the Browns on a pair of Don Cockroft field goals, from 43 and 28 yards, and the Steelers on a Franco Harris one-yard run and a 30-yard field trey by Roy Gerela, making the score 10–6 in favor of Pittsburgh at the half. Brian Sipe, knocked out of the game with a concussion late in the first half, was replaced by World Football League castoff Dave Mays.

Cleo Miller scored from a yard out in the third quarter to give the Browns a 12–10 lead. Cockroft missed the extra point but made up for it with 50- and 40-yard field goals to increase the home team's advantage to 18–10 in the fourth quarter. The Steelers scored a meaningless touchdown late, and the Browns pulled the upset, 18–16.

The Browns' shocking win not only will be remembered for its upset status but also for a play in the fourth quarter in which Jones grabbed Bradshaw in the backfield, flipped him over his head, and slammed him headfirst to the ground near the Browns' sideline. Bradshaw was carried off the field on a stretcher with back and neck injuries, causing him to miss the next two games. Not that it mattered much, but Bradshaw did not lose the ball until he hit the ground, so it was not ruled a fumble.

"All I remember is that Bradshaw always tucked the ball and was ready to run because he was one of the bigger quarterbacks," Thom Darden said. "Joe got to him, and Bradshaw was struggling, trying to get out of his grasp. And Joe just grabbed him, picked him up, and dumped him on his head. Bradshaw was like a chicken with his head cut off. He flopped around. I thought the guy was dead. That could've been a serious blow for him."

Michael Cuomo was sitting right around the 15 or 20 yard line a few rows up. "I thought Bradshaw broke his neck because it looked like his legs were quivering on the field," he said. "I know he was carted off on a gurney, the whole nine yards. But I have to say this—this might show my Steeler hate, but Bradshaw was a drama queen, so you just never knew if he was being dramatic or not."

Added Mike Peticca, "The initial reaction was that you hoped he was okay."

Neither Doug Dieken or Jerry Sherk believed Jones intentionally tried to harm Bradshaw.

"I think Joe just meant to put him on the ground," Dieken said. "Once you finally got your arms around him, and then all of a sudden, his feet are off the ground, then boom! He goes down. That's why they have a lot of these rules today. I do remember they brought Bradshaw into our locker room in the back room to get checked by the doctors. I remember going back there after the game and saying, 'Hello' and saying, 'Are you okay?' He was pretty dazed."

"I can't remember actually seeing it happen," said Sherk, "but from film sessions the way that Joe kind of gobbled Bradshaw up, twisted him at the same time, wrapped his arms around him and threw him back, I think it was not an involuntary reaction but something that he didn't plan. His momentum just took him to that point, and he gave it that extra oomph."

"I was sitting in the bleachers. It was deafening noise," Steve King said. "Did Joe Jones need to take him up and spike him? Probably not, but you couldn't hear the whistle to end the play. When he did that to Bradshaw and Bradshaw hit the ground, he kind of flopped like a fish. I thought he'd broken his back. He hit him that hard. It was thunderous. If that happened now, Jones would probably be in prison, but back then that was the way the game was played, unfortunately. It was rough. Did he need to do that? No, because you could've broken his neck, you could've paralyzed him. I am shocked that he didn't break his neck. I don't think Jones got thrown out of the game. After the game, Turkey went into the medical room between the two locker rooms where they had Bradshaw sequestered to try to see how he was. They had a couple goons in there, probably security people, and they pushed him away, and JoJo Starbuck, Bradshaw's wife at the time, was all upset at Turkey. Turkey had some death threats when the Browns went to Pittsburgh the next year. The play kind of symbolized the physicality of the series. It had gone from rough games to really rough games. I don't know if it was the most physical series in the league at the time, but it was right up there."

13

REGGIE RUCKER: I FINALLY FOUND A HOME

It gets old. You've heard it many times before. The old song and dance.

A professional athlete takes the money and runs. He leaves one team to play for another for bigger bucks, then outright lies to the public about his reason for leaving.

"It's a better fit for me over there."

"I'd like to play for a contending team."

"My wife would like to live in LA."

The list goes on and on, and it gets tiring.

Wouldn't it be nice, novel even, to once—once!—hear a pro athlete admit that more moolah is the reason for a change in teams? It's not as though an athlete changing teams for more money is against the law. Sure, it's going to rub some fans the wrong way, but isn't making as much money as one can the American way?

That is why, although on a much lower scale and under completely different circumstances, what ex-Browns wide receiver Reggie Rucker—a three-sport star in high school—said when asked why he chose to go to the Dallas Cowboys' training camp in 1969 over signing with baseball's Washington Senators, his hometown team, was so refreshing.

"I was broke," Rucker said. "The Cowboys offered me a $250 signing bonus."

Rucker, who played for Cleveland from 1975 to 1981, was born and raised in the southeast section of Washington, DC, an inner-city area not exactly known for country clubs and tea parties.

"It was the projects," he said. "No way out, nothing going on. Drugs and all of that kind of stuff."

Rucker's mother raised him and his bountiful number of half-brothers and sisters by herself. Rucker did his best to stay out of trouble, turning to athletics. He excelled in baseball, football, and basketball at Anacostia High School and was—and still is—friends with former Cleveland Cavaliers great, and current Cavs television color analyst, Austin Carr, who at the same time was an exceptional athlete himself in the southwest section of Washington.

Baseball was Rucker's best sport; he was a five-tool player as a center fielder and received a contract offer from the Senators. However, he decided to take advantage of a new program in which a group of Ivy League schools had created a liaison through their alumni to begin recruiting Washington's metropolitan school systems for African American athletes who had the academic ability to attend not only those schools but other schools as well. It was a movement designed to start a pipeline among alumni of Ivy League schools who had become CEOs of large corporations.

"They were trying to do something with inner-city kids in DC, give them some sort of chance at a future, and I was the first one in the program," Rucker said. "They recognized, I guess, what was in me, they could see a future. They were trying to get me out."

Because he had no father or any kind of father figure around, Rucker was guided by a team of individuals who led him to decline football scholarship offers from big-time programs across the country, including Michigan State University and the University of Colorado, in order to accept a full ride to Boston University.

Although recruited by Boston University as a defensive back, Rucker was soon switched to wide receiver and wing, and he set records as a kick returner for the Terriers. Because the NCAA did not allow freshmen to participate in varsity athletics at the time, Rucker had to wait until his sophomore year in 1966. He helped BU, a Division I program at the time, to 5–5 and 5–3–1 records in 1966 and 1968, respectively, but a 3–6 mark in 1967 was sandwiched in between.

Rucker also played baseball at Boston U., leading the Terriers to two NCAA playoff appearances. In fact, Rucker is one of the rare athletes to be inducted into two Halls of Fame at the same school: He is honored in both the football and baseball shrines at BU.

Rucker was expected to be taken early in the 1969 NFL-AFL Draft. No one chose him, though.

"The Cowboys told me they thought I was going to play baseball," he said.

Dallas brought Rucker to training camp as a free agent cornerback/kick returner that summer. Rucker knew he was a long shot to make the championship-contending team that was stocked with superstars. "I figured I'd take the bonus money, give it a shot, and if I got cut, I could still sign with the Senators and play baseball, which was my best sport anyway," he said.

In a rookie scrimmage against the Oakland Raiders, Rucker got beat for a big play while playing cornerback and fumbled away a punt, too. He thought for sure it was the end of his playing days on the gridiron.

"I thought I was gone," he said.

Then the turning point of Rucker's career occurred.

"Receivers coach [and future Hall of Famer] Raymond Berry," Rucker said, "came up to me that Monday and said, 'Reggie, I've been watching you play cornerback, and I've seen you intercept passes and make catches that not even some of our receivers can make. I've asked [head coach] Tom Landry if he would let me work with you.'"

Rucker had received a reprieve. The Cowboys were going to make him a receiver, a position at which he was not without experience. The problem was, the Cowboys were stacked at the position. Bob Hayes and Lance

Rentzel were the starters. One day in practice, Rucker, a second-teamer—and roommate of fellow rookie Roger Staubach—was suddenly sent on to the field to join the first-teamers by—believe it or not—Hayes.

He yelled, 'Hey, number 13, get in there!'" Rucker remembered. "I was like, 'Me?' So I went on to the field and took my position. Craig Morton audibled, and it was coming to me! I was watching the safety, and the safety blitzed. I broke it off, Morton threw me the ball, and I went about 60 yards all the way for a touchdown. I think that did it for me because—and, remember, that system was very difficult to pick up—Tom Landry was all about, 'How smart are you?' 'How football-sure are you?' The key things on that touchdown play were that I picked up the audible, that I had eye contact with the quarterback, and that I broke off the pattern. To be able to do that as a rookie free agent…"

The Cowboys' veterans took notice, too, and began including Rucker in their off-the-field activities. "They told me, 'Rook, you've got it all. The moves, the speed, the hands, everything," Rucker said. "'You keep doing what you're doing.' I could feel it because I was doing stuff out on the field that I didn't know where it was coming from. I guess my gift was just coming out."

Unfortunately, injuries played a big part throughout Rucker's career, beginning with a broken wrist bone suffered that preseason. He missed most of the season, returning only for the Cowboys' Playoff Bowl loss to the Los Angeles Rams in the 10th annual—and final—matchup of the two conference runners-up.

Rucker suffered another injury in 1970 and, just as he was about to return to action, Rentzel encountered some off-the-field problems, opening the door for Rucker to join the starting lineup. The Cowboys went on a hot streak and did not lose another game until Super Bowl V, when Baltimore beat them on a last-second field goal. Rucker was a starter in that game.

"It was quite a thrill," he said.

Rucker then had major reconstructive surgery on both feet, repairing a congenital problem that plagued him throughout his career. Dallas waived him early in the 1971 season and he spent a month with the New York Giants before being traded to New England. Why did the Cowboys trade him?

"My feet," Rucker said. "Years later, Landry was quoted as saying that I had the worst feet he'd ever seen. He didn't think I would ever play again."

New England was where Rucker met a guy by the name of Sam Rutigliano, the Patriots' receivers coach at the time. As longtime Browns fans know, the two of them would join forces later in the decade and bring much excitement to the North Coast.

The next season, 1972, was when Rucker's career really took off. He led the pitiful Patriots in receptions, receiving yards, and touchdown catches and was voted the team's Most Valuable Player. He had an even better year in 1973, leading the Pats in receptions and receiving yards. Ten games into the 1974 season Rucker suffered a season-ending injury, breaking the same wrist bone he broke five years earlier—but on the other hand. An ugly incident between Rucker and an assistant coach led to Rucker getting traded to the Browns after the season.

Rucker gave the Browns something they desperately needed—a burner at wideout. He led the AFC in 1975 with 60 receptions (the most catches by a Browns player since Mac Speedie in 1952) and led the Browns with 770 receiving yards despite playing inured; he tore up his knee in training camp (prompting another surgery after the season). He also accomplished the feats despite playing on a team that lost its first nine games en route to a 3–11 last-place finish in the AFC Central Division under first-year head coach Forrest Gregg.

"Rucker had that fantastic '75 season," Steve King said, "despite a messed-up quarterback situation and not much on the offensive line. Right away, he was good."

The team began to build around Rucker, drafting Mike Pruitt and Dave Logan and bringing back ex-Brown—and future Hall of Fame receiver—Paul Warfield the next year. Mike Phipps got hurt during the 1976 season opener against the New York Jets. Rucker's take on Phipps's injury and what transpired during the next five seasons?

"Had Phipps not been injured," he said, "you would never have heard of Brian Sipe."

Rucker again the led the Browns in receptions and receiving yards in 1976 and also in touchdown catches, helping the team improve to 9–5, barely missing the playoffs. Warfield was quoted in a newspaper article as saying, "[Rucker's] not doing this because I'm here [and getting double-teamed], he's doing it because he's that good. I've got nothing to do with that guy's success," which Rucker appreciated very much.

Rucker led the Browns in receiving yards for the third straight year in 1977, but a tumble in the second half of the season left the team in last place. Under new head coach Rutigliano, the 1978 Browns won their first three games, the first time in 15 years that had happened, and they finished 8–8. Rucker once again was the go-to guy, hauling in 43 passes for 893 yards for an incredible 20.8 yards per catch average—all team highs. He also totaled a team-best eight touchdown receptions.

Rucker had solid numbers the next year with 43 catches for 749 yards and six touchdown receptions, helping the Kardiac Kids to a 9–7 record, nearly making the playoffs. One of Rucker's most memorable moments that season was a 39-yard touchdown strike he caught from Sipe in overtime in an electrifying victory over the Miami Dolphins in a crucial late-season contest. He was an integral part of the 1980 Browns' Kardiac Kids season with 52 receptions, 768 receiving yards, and four touchdown catches. The season ended in disappointment in the "Red Right 88" playoff game against Oakland.

Expectations were skyrocketing as the 1981 season approached. The Browns, however, slipped to 5–11 and a last-place finish. Rucker, though, still managed to catch 27 balls for 532 yards. He decided to call it quits just days before the 1982 season opener.

"These days," said Mike Peticca, "maybe Rucker would be an ideal slot receiver. As far as defining a position, I don't think they had that in those days. You had basically the two wideouts and the tight end. He wasn't known for blazing speed, but he had a real knack for getting open. He really ran precise routes and had very good hands. He certainly seemed to be unafraid of taking a hit. He was good then, and he might be even better these days with that precise of a role. He was a clutch receiver, too. I doubt he had many drops in key situations."

"He was fantastic," King said. "When Sam came, he became even better. He did a great job. He kind of became a go-to guy on those Kardiac Kids teams. He had great hands. He was a great receiver."

"He was a hell of a good wide receiver," said Dan Coughlin.

Rucker delved into the broadcast booth as a television analyst for Browns preseason games until they left for Baltimore and broadcast NFL games on NBC from 1983 to 1989. He also partnered with Joe Tait in calling Cleveland Indians games on WUAB TV-43 in 1983 and 1984. Rucker called Mid-American Conference football games for SportsChannel America for two years before venturing into radio in 1991 as one of the original sports talk show hosts on Cleveland's WKNR AM-1220 (now WKNR AM-850). He also was a Browns analyst on WEWS Channel 5's Sunday evening *Sports Sunday* show for several years.

Rucker then decided to leave sports media and went into the investment business to become a stockbroker. He did that for some 10 years. He was also the executive director of an organization called Cleveland Sports Stars that raised money for children's cancer research for about 15 years. He also served as the alumni liaison—in which he advised Carmen Policy on the Browns' legacy and the Cleveland community—for the reborn Browns from 1999 to 2005. He was responsible for originally coming up with the idea of starting the Browns Legends, a sort of Browns Hall of Fame that inducts different players each year, in 2001. He also authored a book published in 2002 entitled *From Ghetto to God: The Incredible Journey of NFL Star, Reggie Rucker.*

The 77-year-old Rucker was the executive director of Jim Browns's Amer-I-Can program and also was the president of the Peacemakers Alliance, ex-Mayor Frank Jackson's initiative for outreach and working with at-risk youth in the city of Cleveland.

Rucker also believes in the current regime running the Browns.

"I think they're going to get it right," he said.

Getting it right was something Rucker did repeatedly throughout his 13-year playing career.

"I was always a player who I think delivered," he said.

Indeed he did—in the form of 310 receptions, 4,953 receiving yards, and 32 touchdown catches in his seven seasons with the Browns and a total of 447 receptions, 7,065 receiving yards, and 44 touchdown catches in his NFL career.

Not bad for an undrafted free agent. With bad feet.

14

GIB SHANLEY: THE VOICE OF THE BROWNS

The name "Gib Shanley" was synonymous with Cleveland Browns football the same way Santa Claus is synonymous with Christmas, the way Johnny Carson was synonymous with late-night television comedy, or the way pepperoni is synonymous with pizza. Shanley was the Browns' radio play-by-play announcer from 1961 to 1984, teaming with Jim Graner from 1963 through 1974 and Jim Mueller from 1975 through 1984. Shanley also worked in Cleveland television, first as a weekend sportscaster at WKYC Channel 3 and then as sports director on WEWS Channel 5. His duties at WEWS would also later include hosting a weekly Browns highlights show called *Quarterback Club* until 1976. The Bellaire, Ohio, native, however, was known mostly for his work on the Browns' radio broadcasts. He had many admirers, including Mike Peticca.

"I thought Gib was the absolute best," he said, "and I don't mean just among Cleveland guys but among anyone I've heard in any sport, and I don't say that lightly. As far as listening to him for the game experience, he was the guy. Maybe there are other guys right there, but I can't think of anyone better just for the experience of listening to the game and how he impacted what you were feeling about the game. He was really good at picking the spots to amp the volume. Just on radio, it seemed like there was a real connection, him and the listener. Some guys you hear, and you kind of feel separated. He had a real knack for making the listener feel like he was really describing it for you. I think he was the best at setting up the play and describing the play. After a big play would happen, he wouldn't immediately rush into whatever further description or more explanation of how big the play was or whatever. He was really good at just letting the crowd noise stand alone as to the significance of what had just happened with the play. He'd just let you hear the crowd for a few seconds sometimes. He'd pick what seemed like the very right spot to start talking again. He was an expert at picking the spots. I think a good thing about that era was that the announcers didn't have these prepared, little, 'trademark' things they wanted to say like there are now. It was enjoyable to hear Gib. You almost felt like a part of the crowd there."

"Gib was so good," said Steve King. "He was the first guy for whom you'd turn down the sound on the TV and you'd turn up the sound on the radio. You had a picture of what was going on in your head, you could see it by Gib Shanley. He painted such a picture. Gib understood the game. You could see everything going on. When Gib Shanley said it, you knew it to be true. He understood the radio medium, that these people weren't seeing what I was seeing. You needed to have somebody paint a picture, and he did. It was great. It was like you were at the game. It was unbelievable. He was so good at what he did. He was as good of a radio play-by-play guy as there ever was because he understood what he needed to do. He was fantastic. In 1984 in the preseason opener against Pittsburgh, the Browns had brown jerseys with orange numbers. Gib bitched from the time he saw them until the time the game ended about how he couldn't read the numbers. Guess what? Those orange numbers went away. In the '70s, Gib went down to Ohio State when they needed a temporary replacement at play-by-play and did a couple Buckeyes games and was just as good."

Shanley was also a very witty guy. "He was doing one of the early games that he announced, and the Browns had been shut out in the first half," said Bob Dolgan, former longtime sports columnist for *The Plain Dealer.* "When they trotted off the field Shanley said, 'That's the first time the Browns have crossed the 50 yard line all day.' Art Modell came down on him and said, 'I never want to hear that kind of stuff again.' At that time, the owners of the teams had complete approval rights over who announced their games. If an owner didn't want a local sportscaster doing his games, all he had to do was tell the radio station. So the sportscasters were virtually Browns employees. Modell particularly didn't like people making fun of his product. Shanley, knowing which side of the bread was buttered, naturally became a huge ally of Modell, and if you were on his side, he was a very good guy to know. Shanley was his main spokesman. And every time I'd write a column criticizing Modell, Shanley several times on his sports news broadcasts would rip me by name and say, 'I don't understand why *The Plain Dealer* continues to pay this man.'"

Shanley enjoyed gambling a little bit, too, and he would even put a bet down on the Browns occasionally. "We were playing in Atlanta in 1976," Dan Coughlin recalled. "The week of our game with the Falcons, Marion Campbell, their head coach, gets fired, so many members of the staff quit in protest and in sympathy and in support. So we're down there in the hotel in Atlanta, and who comes over to visit his old media guys from Cleveland but former Browns quarterback Bill Nelsen, who's Atlanta's quarterbacks coach? He's telling us how that team, Atlanta, is in a shambles, that morale on the team is terrible and how everybody's in confusion. So I'm thinking, 'Boy, this is a time to put a bet on a game.' I wasn't much of a gambler then, but I'm thinking, 'Man.' It's about midnight, and Nelsen leaves us. I go up to my room and I call my gambling contact. I said, 'I'd like to get $500 down on the Browns tomorrow.' I'd never made a bet like that in my life. The Browns were favored by maybe three-and-a-half points. He says, 'Okay, you know if you lose, you're gonna owe $550.' I said, 'Okay.' The game was played on a misty day, and the ball was a little bit slippery. The Browns screw it up at the end. Mike Phipps had been recovering from a separated shoulder, and this was his first game back after the injury. He didn't play quarterback; he came in to hold on the kicks to get him some game action. It's late in the game, a minute-and-a-half left or something. We're ahead by three points, and we lined up for a field goal to give us a six-point cushion. Phipps fumbles the snap. We never get the field goal off and I lose 550 bucks. We're leaving the press box to go down into the locker room to get my postgame interviews. Gib is wrapping up his postgame show, and he comes out of the broadcast booth. I can tell on his face from his expression that 'my god, he *also* bet on the Browns.' I had never seen a longer face in my life than Gib Shanley's expression walking out of that press box that day. Wow!"

In February 1985, Shanley resigned from his post at WEWS and decided to move to California to continue his career on the advice from his good friend Ernie Anderson, who lived there and did some work for ABC television. Remembered Dolgan, "Ernie said, 'The Rams are going to need a new play-by-play guy because Bob Starr is going to retire. And you can make a hell of a lot of money out here.' But Starr decided not to retire, so Gib is out there with no job and an angry wife. However, in the middle of the 1985 season, Starr has a heart attack, and Gib gets to be his temporary fill-in guy for several games, but he made no impact on the listening audience in Los Angeles. Starr came back, and Gib never got the full-time job with the Rams."

"Everybody and their uncle tried to talk him out of moving to California," King said, "but he did it anyway."

"Of course, nobody knew who Gib was in California, so he had trouble getting steady work," Dolgan said. "He'd gone out there with his wife, and she didn't want to leave town, but he talked her into it. She got a real good job in advertising or marketing or something. I was doing a radio-TV column then, and I'd call him from time to time and say, 'How are things going?' He was always cordial and we'd have a conversation. The last time I called him I said, 'What are you doing out there? Anybody hiring you?' He said, 'No, not really. Last week I had a job substituting for one night or two nights for somebody. I'm just raking the leaves out here.' I said, 'So how's your wife doing?' He said, 'Oh, she's doing great. She loves it here.' I said, 'No kidding?' He said, 'I think I'm going to come back to Cleveland.' I said, 'What about your wife?' He said, 'Well, she's going to stay here.' I said, 'What??? You mean you're getting a divorce?' He said, 'Yes, we are.'"

Shanley eventually did return to Cleveland with his tail between his legs, becoming sports director for WUAB-TV Channel 43's then fledgling 10 p.m. weeknight newscast in 1988, which he continued to do until 1996. That year, he became guest commentator on the weekly sports wrap-up/NFL coverage and commentary show, *Countdown to 99*, that was hosted by Casey Coleman and Reggie Rucker. In the 2000s, Shanley served as a commentator on WEWS's sports wrap-up show, *Sports Sunday*.

But what Shanley, who passed away on April 6, 2008, will be most remembered for by Cleveland fans were his sensational calls of Browns games on the radio.

"Gib set the play, just told you every little detail that was going on," said Mike McLain. "It was simplicity with him like Ray Scott did with the Packers. 'Rya-a-an … Collins, got it. Touchdown.' Gib was the ultimate pro."

15

PHIPPS FOR NEWSOME ... THAT'S HOW IT TURNED OUT!

The Browns made a number of positive trades and not so positive trades throughout the 1970s. Perhaps the best trade they made came on May 3, 1977, when they shipped Mike Phipps to Chicago in exchange for the Bears' first-round pick in 1978. The Browns used that selection to pick Ozzie Newsome with the 23rd overall selection in the '78 draft. Other than a 9–1 record as the starter in 1979, Phipps did not do much in his five seasons in the "Windy City." Newsome, meanwhile, went on to a Hall of Fame career in 13 seasons with the Browns. He led the Browns in receptions and receiving yards every season from 1981 to 1985. He topped 1,000 yards receiving twice, in 1981 and 1983. He was voted to three Pro Bowls. With the "Wizard of Oz" now in town via the Phipps deal the year before, the horrendous trade eight years earlier that sent Paul Warfield to the Miami Dolphins and brought Phipps to Cleveland had come full circle.

Another trade that worked in the Browns' favor came when, on January 28, 1975, they dealt a fourth-round draft choice that year to New England for Reggie Rucker.

With the fourth-rounder, the Patriots selected University of Southern California running back Allen Carter. Carter rushed the ball just 22 times for 95 yards for the Patriots that season, then appeared in only one game in 1976, returning one kickoff for 19 yards. Rucker, on the other hand, enjoyed seven productive seasons in Cleveland. He was the team leader in receptions in 1975, 1976, and 1978, receiving yards every year from 1975 to 1978, and touchdown receptions in 1976 and 1978. As a Brown, he caught 310 passes for 4,953 yards, including numerous clutch grabs.

One of the worst trades not only in the 1970s but in Browns history was when, on January 26, 1970, they shipped Paul Warfield to the Dolphins in exchange for the third pick in the following day's NFL draft. The Browns used the pick on Mike Phipps from Purdue University. A sensational six-year veteran at the time of the trade, Warfield had given Browns fans innumerable thrills with his artistry on the field. Warfield in action was Picasso with a paintbrush, Spielberg with a script. He was fast, fearless, and agile, with great hands and moves that left defenders in a trance. Other than the 1965 season in which he missed 10 games due to a preseason shoulder injury, Warfield averaged an astounding 20.7 yards per catch from 1964 to 1969, a period in which the Browns played in four NFL championship games, winning one. He led the team in receiving yardage in four of those years and, in 1968, became the first Cleveland player to achieve 1,000 yards receiving (1,067) since Mac Speedie in 1949.

While the 1970 Warfield-less Browns failed to qualify for postseason play for the first time in four years, Warfield led the Dolphins to their first playoff berth ever that season. The years that followed saw Cleveland plummet to the depths of despair and Miami ascend to greatness, topped off by two straight Super Bowl titles in 1972 and 1973. While Phipps turned out to be a first-rate flop whose best year as a Brown came in 1972 when he had 13 touchdown passes and 16 interceptions, Warfield went on to lead the Dolphins in receiving yards every year from 1970 to 1973. Warfield, who closed out his career back in Cleveland in 1976 and 1977, would go on to be enshrined into the Pro Football Hall of Fame in 1983.

Another trade that did not go in the Browns' favor was when, on May 3, 1979, they dealt a first-round choice that year to San Diego for first- and second-round picks that year. With the Chargers' first-rounder, the 20th overall pick, the Browns selected wide receiver Willis Adams from the University of Houston. Adams turned out to be a major disappointment, catching just 61 balls for less than 1,000 yards in seven seasons. With the second-rounder, Cleveland chose University of Oklahoma offensive tackle Sam Claphan, who missed the 1979 season with a back injury and was released the next year. With the Browns' first-round pick, the Chargers took a tight end out of the University of Missouri by the name of Kellen Winslow Sr.

Enough said.

We offer you a bonus trade the Browns made on August 26, 1974, that really favored neither team. The deal was pretty much a stalemate. The Browns shipped a wide receiver to New Orleans who had already signed to play for the Jacksonville Sharks of the World Football League and never played a down for the Saints. New Orleans sent a wide receiver to the Browns who spent only the 1974 season with Cleveland and had only six catches for 74 yards. What made the deal so unforgettable then? The players' names. The receiver the Browns obtained from the Saints was a guy with the jazzy sounding name of Jubilee Dunbar. The wideout the Saints got from the Browns? A guy by the name of Fair Hooker.

"Fair Hooker" is a hard name to miss. "Dandy" Don Meredith declared on the first Monday Night Football telecast, "I've never met a fair hooker (prompting stone silence from the usually loquacious Howard Cosell)." Hooker, a Browns wide receiver from 1969 to 1974, was not a bad football player. He may not have been Paul Warfield, but he had a nice career with the Browns.

Players would poke fun at Hooker's unique name when they first met him, according to Hooker, who now lives in Inglewood, California, "but then they got used to it," he said. A fifth-round draft pick by Cleveland in 1969 out of Arizona State University, Hooker caught 28 passes for 490 yards in 1970. He had his finest year ever the next season when he had 45 receptions for 649 yards. Hooker's numbers began to decline in 1972, but he still had 32 catches for 441 yards that year.

16

LUNCH-PAIL PLAYERS

Imagine Deshaun Watson selling insurance. Imagine Amari Cooper as a construction worker. Think of Myles Garrett showing up at your house with a carpet-cleaning business. Think about that. Hard to contemplate? Of course. After all, why would those three Browns players work those "menial" jobs when they are multimillionaires from playing professional football?

There was a time, however, when pro athletes did not make the mega bucks today's athletes make, when they made not much more than the average Joe. And that time was the 1970s. Most athletes back then worked offseason jobs to supplement their income from whatever sport they played. The Browns of the '70s were no different. Most of their players had to work offseason jobs to make ends meet.

"That's the way it was, and the players knew it, they understood it," Steve King said. "It had been that way through pro football forever. Dante Lavelli with the appliance company. Lou Groza got into insurance. There [were] all kinds of stuff the players did. There was no union to speak of. The strikes that they had in '74 …

those were things that were needed to kind of get the game where that big pot of gold was being split up. But until that started to happen and was substantiated, they needed to go work somewhere in the offseason."

Doug Dieken worked as a substitute teacher at his high school and grade school early in his career. "Substitute teaching was an interesting experience. Basically, if you're a substitute teacher, you're a babysitter for an hour for each class," he said. "High school wasn't bad, but in grade school those kids would challenge you. In grade school it was a class of kids that were disruptive. This one kid is screwing around, and I said, 'Get up here! Give me 25 sit-ups.' I found out the kid liked the attention, so then I had him do some push-ups and some more sit-ups. Then the bell rang, and the kid left. I had a free period, so I went into the coaches office and sat in there for a while. Then the bell rang for the next class, and this coach comes into the classroom and said, 'Hey, you almost killed that kid.' I said, 'What are you talking about?' He said, 'You know you had him doing those sit-ups and push-ups?' I said, 'Yeah?' He said, 'He had swimming class the next period. He cramped up.' I said, 'Oh-h-h shit!'

"When you came back to the team after the offseason, they had a questionnaire you had to fill out and one of the questions was, 'What did you do in the offseason?' And one of the high-school substitute-teaching classes I taught was German. I had taken German in high school, but I didn't know squat as far as *speaking* German. So I wrote down that I taught German in the offseason. And I got one of my bubblegum cards later on, and it says, 'He taught German in the offseason.' It sounds good, but it isn't what it says.

"Then I worked for the government in which I tried to find summer jobs for minority students. I did that for two or three years. Then Gene Hickerson and I formed a company that sold soak pit covers, which lasted about a year."

Gary Collins worked in the horse breeding business. "It was my first wife's love," he said. "We had the appaloosas and we bred the mares to the top stallions all over the country. My last two years, I had a radio show. I gave sports commentary. If I'd pursued it, I'd have been in the radio business when I quit football."

Billy Andrews went home to Louisiana and, with his brother, ran a dairy farm that they inherited from their father. Meanwhile, Fred Hoaglin mainly worked as a stockbroker for McDonald & Co., a brokerage firm in Cleveland.

Thom Darden worked during the offseason not because he did not make enough money playing football but mostly because he was trying to figure out what he wanted to do once his football career was done.

"I didn't really think about the money," he said.

Darden went to John Carroll University (JCU) and earned his degree that he had started at the University of Michigan, and then he worked at JCU for two years as assistant financial aid director. He then worked at Republic Steel for a couple years in the personnel department and helped with tours of the steel mill. "Then Art Modell," he said, "referred me to WHK Radio 1420-AM, the home of the Browns, where I worked in the sales department and sold advertising on the Browns' broadcasts. I really got a lot of good experience in the advertising business. WHK's sister station was WMMS 100.7-FM, a rock station, on which I had a Sunday night jazz show, 'All-Pro Jazz,' which was actually year-round for two years. Then three other guys and I built a cable television system in East Cleveland. One of my partners eventually bought me out."

Jerry Sherk was one of the few Browns players in the 1970s who never worked an offseason job during his playing days. "I had enough money to live on," he said. "My first contract was $18,000, $20,000, and $22,000 per year. That's when a good living wage would've been $6,000 per year, so I was probably making three times what the average person was making. Plus, I got a little bonus. I was so focused on becoming a better football player. I went back to school and studied psychology and I studied athletic transition. Athletic transition is a body of work that tries to support athletes as they move from their sport to private life whether it be Olympic, college, high school, or professional. They call it the life jacket syndrome. A life jacket is an offseason job. But what you want to do as an athlete is become the best. So in that scenario, you don't want a life jacket because you want to be the best swimmer. You don't want that lifejacket to take the edge off of your need to perform as a football player. So I was one of those guys. I worked out and just thought about the game a lot. I always analyzed at the end of the season how my year was, what I was good at, what I needed to improve on, and how to improve. So I never got a job in the offseason. When I got hurt later in my career, there were times in the locker room where I felt like I wasn't being productive, but I had to kind of hang around the locker room. And that's when I picked up a camera. And I learned from the United Press International [UPI] and Associated Press photographers. So that kind of developed into my second career. Sometimes in my last couple offseasons, I worked a little bit for UPI. Then, when I left the Browns, I was a professional photographer for seven or eight years."

Another way Browns players in the late 1970s and into the early 1980s made extra cash was by doing something all of the NFL teams were doing then—playing basketball. "The Browns had an offseason basketball team that played various faculty and alumni teams, and they drew huge crowds," King said. "They could make money. They needed to make money."

"We even played Big Chuck and Lil' John," Dieken said. "We made a little money for it, but the rest of the money was used as fundraiser money for the schools. It was a great way to stay in shape, too."

17

THE "OTHER" PRUITT

The first time Mike Pruitt ran on to the Cleveland Municipal Stadium field for a regular- season game, he was in awe. The Browns were playing the New York Jets. The Jets quarterback was Joe Namath.

"I was thinking, 'I can't believe I'm actually here, competing with guys who I've watched for years!'" the former Browns fullback recalled. "And the Cleveland fans were remarkable. I'd never seen anything like it."

Pruitt went on to enjoy a successful nine-year career with Cleveland. He was shocked when the Browns selected him seventh overall in the 1976 NFL draft out of Purdue University. Pruitt expected to be drafted but not that high.

"Maybe in the second or third round," he said.

Pruitt got off to a rough start under head coach Forrest Gregg. He sat on the bench much of the time and was starting to doubt his abilities. When Sam Rutigliano came aboard as head coach in 1978, things changed. Rutigliano believed in Pruitt and gave him his chance to shine. On October 29 of that season, Pruitt's career turned around. He scored on a 71-yard run that helped the Browns to a 41–20 victory over Buffalo.

"That gave me the confidence boost I desperately needed," he said. "For the first time, I truly believed I belonged in the NFL."

Belong he did. Pruitt led the Browns in rushing yards every year from 1979 to 1983, topping the 1,000-yard mark every season in that span except the strike-shortened 1982 campaign. Pruitt was a Pro Bowler in 1979 and 1980.

"Sam told me that Pruitt's hands never were tremendous," Steve King said, "but the coaches gave him enough confidence and worked with him on catching the ball that he was adept enough at catching the ball and became a weapon out of the backfield. In 1977 you would've never predicted that. He looked like a flop. 'You wasted a draft pick on this guy who can't hold on to the ball?' The more they played him, the worse it got because he kept fumbling. Forrest Gregg broke him because Mike Pruitt needed somebody to love him. That's what Sam did. He worked with him and built up his confidence. Pruitt got to the point where he could be a pretty good receiver coming out of the backfield. He was as good of a back as there was for that period of time. He really was. He was strong, he was tough, he caught the ball out of the backfield. And it was all because of working with him technique-wise. He gained the confidence that he could catch the ball. Sam said his hands never became great, but they became good enough."

"Pruitt struggled his first couple years and had a fumbling problem early on," said Mike Peticca, "but between the tackles, he was just dynamite, and yet he had the speed to get outside. He had no showboat attitude to him at all. He was probably underrated among his contemporaries even though his numbers were so good. I think once he maybe got over confidence problems and became established, he was just outstanding. He was known to not have great hands as a receiver, but he wasn't bad at that. He was a legitimate Pro Bowl type running back for several years. I remember him as a good blocker, too. He was perfect for that offense just as a complement to the passing game."

"Mike was very powerful, very muscular," said Jerry Sherk. "He seemed to have a fumbling problem for a year or two, and Coach Gregg kind of roasted him for that. He might've become a little more tentative. But when he hit his speed, he did a tremendous job. He was so powerful that if you stuck your arm out there, you felt like he was going to rip it off because he went through the hole so powerfully."

"Mike Pruitt was just the opposite of Greg Pruitt and was very good at it," Mike McLain said. "He was the ground machine."

Added Doug Dieken, "Mike was a power runner, a straight-line, see-hole, run-hole back."

Pruitt said the Kardiac Kids days were the most thrilling times he had in Cleveland— moments like the Monday night shocker over the Cowboys in a rocking Cleveland Stadium in 1979, the upset of the Oilers in the Astrodome the next year, and the division clincher three weeks later in Cincinnati.

There were also moments Pruitt would like to file away forever, such as the excruciating loss to the Minnesota Vikings a week before the Bengals game that nearly cost the Browns a playoff berth.

"The worst one, though, should come as no surprise to Browns fans," he grimly recalled. "Red Right 88."

Whether pleasant memories or not, Pruitt, 70, will always hold a special place in his heart for the orange and brown.

"I'll always cherish my days with the Browns," he said.

18

DON COCKROFT: AS STEADY AS THEY COME

It was Thanksgiving Day 1966. The Cockroft family was visiting relatives in Nebraska, near Omaha. Everyone was gathered around the television watching one of three pro football games on the docket that day – the Browns against the Dallas Cowboys in the Cotton Bowl.

"We're sitting there watching this on a black and white TV," Don Cockroft recalled. "I remember Lou Groza kicked off, and my dad said, 'Son, if you could just get that old man to teach you how to kick, I think you might make it.'"

Little did Cockroft, whose college playing days were coming to a close, know that less than two years later his father's wish would come true. Cockroft was drafted by the Browns in 1967, and by 1968, he had supplanted Groza as Cleveland's kicker. The Browns kept "The Toe" on as Cockroft's personal kicking coach for a couple of seasons.

"I got taught by the master," Cockroft said.

Cockroft's long road to the NFL started in the small town of Fountain, Colorado, near Colorado Springs.

Born in Cheyenne, Wyoming, Cockroft and his family moved to a small farm some two-and-a-half hours south of Denver when he was four years old. The Cockrofts—Don was the middle son of five boys—moved to Fountain the summer before he was to begin eighth grade.

"I'd been on the seventh-grade football team our last year on the farm," Cockroft said, "but I didn't play much."

His football career really began at Fountain Junior High, where he played wide receiver and defensive back for two years. In high school he was the starting quarterback and middle linebacker, and also played some wideout.

Oh, another thing. Cockroft also had been kicking since the eighth grade.

"Nobody could kick the ball further than me, even my brother, who was four years older than me," Cockroft said. "God blessed me with a lot of snap and a pop in my right leg that was kind of unusual. Kicking, though, never became a main focus for me until college."

Adams State College in Alamosa, Colorado, an NAIA school at the time, was next.

"That was the only school," Cockroft said, "that promised me if I made the team, it'd give me a [partial] scholarship, which I needed to even go to college."

So Cockroft packed his bags in the summer of 1963 and left for Alamosa, hoping to make the Adams State team as a walk-on at quarterback. It didn't take long for

Cockroft to conclude that playing quarterback was not in his future. On top of that, he was homesick.

"I called my mom and asked if I could come home," he said. "Fortunately, she said, 'Son, no, you're not coming home. Do not quit, do not give up. Just do the best you can, and the rest will take care of itself.'"

That is when Cockroft realized that nobody on the team was kicking exceptionally well.

"So I began to focus a lot on my kicking," he said.

Cockroft is a man of strong Christian faith, and has been since he was 13 years old.

"I was hoping and praying that somehow I would make the team as a kicker," he said. "The coach came to me and another guy and said, 'You guys each kick 100 extra points—25 the next four nights—and whoever makes the most is going to be my kicker.' The other guy was a better kicker than me, and he kind of figured he had it made. I think I made about five more extra points than he did."

The coach honored his word. Cockroft became the freshman team's kicker and punter. The next season, he joined the varsity squad. Cockroft, who doubled as the right safety his senior year, was actually a much better punter than kicker in college, as his four-year punting average was an exceptional 44.5 yards. He led the nation—including NCAA Division I schools—during his senior year with an unbelievable 48-yard average.

"I bet I didn't kick 15 field goals in my four years in

college," he laughed. "I literally kept the suspense in the extra point."

Whatever Cockroft did, it was enough to be chosen as the kicker for the North team in the annual North-South Shrine Game in Miami's Orange Bowl his senior year, and also for the following summer's College All-Star Game in Chicago against the defending Super Bowl champion Green Bay Packers.

"As it turned out, I had a very good Shrine Game," he said.

When Cockroft was drafted by the Browns, there was no ESPN, no internet.

"I got a phone call from Art Modell," he said. "Modell said, 'We just drafted you in the third round.'"

The first thing Cockroft did upon hanging up the phone?

"I went to find the atlas, saying to myself, 'Where is Cleveland, Ohio?' Here I was in Alamosa, Colorado, and I look at that stinkin' map of the US and I said, 'Man, that's a long way from home!'"

After a year on the Browns' taxi squad watching and learning from Groza, who, like Cockroft, was also a straight-on kicker—and a stint with the Akron Vulcans, a sort of minor-league team to the NFL—Cockroft was primed and ready to boot Groza out of the Browns' kicking position in 1968. He will never forget the second-to-last—and the only home—preseason game that summer.

"We were playing the Packers in the second game of a doubleheader," he said.

Cockroft was aware this was make-it-or-break-it time for him.

"It was a beautiful, beautiful night," he said. "And eighty-some thousand [84,918] fans were there. I mean, I just got goose bumps standing there during the national anthem, realizing where I was and the opportunity I had. I was so scared and nervous."

Cockroft overcame his jitters and kicked three field goals.

"We got beat, 31–9," he said, "but I was the happiest guy in Cleveland."

The 23-year-old Cockroft had won the kicking job. He celebrated for five minutes or so, then realized, "I'm the kicker for the Cleveland Browns!"

Cockroft had some big shoes to fill in replacing Groza, Cleveland's kicker for 21 of the franchise's 22 years of existence, who would be inducted into the Pro Football Hall of Fame six years later. Cockroft doubled as the Browns' punter for nine seasons, unusual in that most teams at the time were shifting to more specialization, from one player both kicking and punting to two players, one doing the kicking and one doing the punting.

Cockroft joined a Browns team that was used to success. Just four years earlier, the Browns had won the NFL championship, and the year after that they had played in the title game. The team had had just one losing season, in 1956. The Browns continued their winning ways after Cockroft joined the team. They won the Century Division title in both 1968 and 1969, beat Dallas in the playoffs both years, but lost in the NFL championship game both times.

In 1970 the Browns lost the great Paul Warfield in a trade for the right to draft Mike Phipps, and missed the playoffs for the first time in four years. That same season brought *Monday Night Football* into living rooms across the nation. Cockroft and the Browns hosted the very first MNF game, a 31–21 victory over Joe Namath and the New York Jets.

"I look back," Cockroft chuckled, "and jokingly say, 'You know, I had the opening kickoff, the first field goal, the first extra point, the first missed field goal, and the first shanked punt in the history of *Monday Night Football*.'"

Cockroft and the Browns returned to the playoffs in 1971 and 1972, losing in the divisional round both years. Cockroft experienced the most memorable individual moment of his career during the '72 season, on November 19 against the Pittsburgh Steelers in Cleveland Municipal Stadium. The Steelers, finally on the rise after nearly 40 years of failure, were 7–2. The Browns, an aging team soon to be on the decline, were 6–3. The turnpike rivals were meeting at the crossroads in a battle for the AFC Central Division lead. The Browns, assisted by two Cockroft field goals, seemed in control of the game, leading 20–3 in the second quarter. The Steelers cut it to 20-10 at halftime, but another Cockroft field goal made it 23–10 in the third quarter. The Steelers pulled within 23–17 entering the fourth quarter, then a rookie by the name of Franco Harris rumbled 75 yards for a touchdown to give Pittsburgh a 24–23 lead.

Phipps marched the Browns down the field and, with little more than two minutes remaining, Cockroft was sent in to try a 27-yard field goal that, if successful, would have given the Browns the lead. Cockroft had a phenomenal season that year, getting voted Offensive Most Valuable Player of the team and kicking a career-long 57-yard field goal against the Broncos in Denver just three weeks earlier.

"I never prayed so hard in my life," he said. "It was a muddy, nasty field that day, but basically the snap and hold were good. I kicked the ball, and I pulled up, looked up too quick. I wanted to see it go through the uprights."

What Cockroft saw was not a pretty sight.

"That ball missed by about two inches to the right," he said. "And only the Pittsburgh Steelers were yelling and screaming. The rest of that stadium was dead silent. It was the most devastating moment of my career because it was such an important kick."

"Don was a very religious guy … except when he missed a field goal," Doug Dieken said. "The words weren't quite as religious as they normally were."

After the missed field goal, Cockroft returned to the sideline head down.

"Billy Andrews came over and said, 'Don, get your chin up,'" Cockroft recalled. "'We're gonna get the ball back. We're gonna give you a second chance.'"

The Browns did get the ball back.

"I think Nick Roman and Jerry Sherk sacked Terry Bradshaw on third down," Cockroft said. "And, if I'm not mistaken, Leroy Kelly returned the punt to about the 50. There were about two minutes left. I knew if we could get a couple first downs, I'd get a second chance. I literally prayed, 'God, I'll keep my head down, please give me a second chance.' Now, I realize there are Christians on both sides of the ball. But all I know is, I got that second chance."

Cockroft was sent on to the field with 13 seconds left to try a 26-yard field goal with more than 83,000 fans' hearts-a-pounding.

"Unbelievably," Cockroft said, "the ball was within inches of where it was before when I missed."

This time, Cockroft kept his head down.

"I drove the ball and, before I looked up, I said, 'It's gotta be good!' I tell people I saw heaven that day because that sucker sailed dead center through the uprights."

The Browns won, 26–24.

Just how difficult was it to kick and punt on a muddy Cleveland Municipal Stadium field?

"Let's put it this way," Cockroft said. "Every time Jan

Stenerud and Garo Yepremian walked into that stadium, they just shook their heads and said, 'I don't know how you kick in this place.' And when Tom Skladany was drafted by the Browns out of Ohio State in 1977, he refused to play in Cleveland.":

Cockroft and the Browns fell on hard times not long after the 1972 season. They dropped to 7–5–2 in 1973 and won just seven games combined in 1974 and 1975. The team rebounded to 9–5 in 1976 and began 1977 at 5–2 and in first place before the season unraveled into a 6–8 last-place disaster.

The '77 season also brought Cockroft less playing time. He no longer assumed the punting duties and, not surprisingly, he thought it was a bad decision.

"I believed I could still punt the football," he said. "I hung the ball very, very high. Ray Guy was the only punter during my career who I felt could out-punt me."

From the rubble and ruins of 1977's miserable conclusion came a refreshing new head coach in Sam Rutigliano, and the Kardiac Kids were soon to be born. There were glimpses of it in 1978. Then in 1979 the Kardiac in Cleveland really took off. "That's when we started saying, 'Wow! Maybe we've got something going!'" Cockroft said.

A 4–0 start in '79 ended in a 9–7 finish and nearly a playoff berth. After a perplexing 0–2 start in 1980, the Browns won 11 of their last 14 games, most in thrilling fashion, and won the Central Division crown.

One exciting win that Cockroft, who fought through torturous knee problems that year, will never forget was a 27–26 win in Week 8 over the two-time defending Super Bowl champion Steelers at Cleveland Stadium.

"We tied the game at 26 midway through the fourth quarter," Cockroft recalled. "That was the toughest extra point I ever kicked. There was a lot of pressure."

Cockroft was instrumental in Cleveland's division-clinching victory in Cincinnati on the final Sunday of the regular season. He kicked two field goals, including what turned out to be the game-winner from 22 yards with about 1:25 to go in the game. It was Cockroft's 17th career game-winning kick (including extra points) in 17 tries.

Every longtime Browns fan knows what happened two weeks later in the infamous "Red Right 88" playoff game against the Oakland Raiders. Rutigliano eschewed a 30-yard field goal attempt by Cockroft, who admittedly had had a rough day on the icy field, and instead chose to run another play with less than a minute remaining. "When the offense went back on the field," Cockroft recalled, "I said, 'Brian [Sipe], get the ball on the right hashmark.'"

Cockroft was positive he would soon be trotting onto the field to attempt a probable game-winning field goal.

"No ifs, ands, or buts about it," he said.

What happened next haunts Browns fans to this day. Sipe dropped back to pass! He threw the ball into the wicked winds toward Ozzie Newsome in the left corner of the end zone, but Raiders strong safety Mike Davis cut in front of the "Wizard of Oz" and intercepted the ball, closing the book on the Kardiac Kids.

"Cockroft was so hurt during that playoff game against Oakland with different injuries," remembered Mike Peticca. "I wonder how much Sam's decision to pass the ball played into Cockroft's health at that point. It was also terrible conditions to kick. I never thought they should've kicked in that situation. I'm sure they would've kicked on fourth down, and I would've agreed with that."

The next summer, Cockroft was somehow beaten out of the kicking job by a guy named Dave Jacobs. Cockroft hung around and stayed in shape just in case the Browns wanted him back. Jacobs failed miserably and was cut after five games, but the Browns instead traded for Matt Bahr, and the rest is history. Cockroft called it quits. When he retired, he had the highest career field goal percentage (65.9) in NFL history.

"The lineage of the great kickers in franchise history … Cockroft is right there with Lou Groza to Matt Bahr to Matt Stover to Phil Dawson," said Steve King. "Here's a guy who had to follow Lou 'The Toe' Groza, who played with the team for 21 years. The college kicking award is named after Lou Groza. Talk about a tough act to follow. He did a great job following a legend. Cockroft struggled a little bit at the beginning of his career, but when he made that kick against Pittsburgh in '72, then all of a sudden from that time on he was as good as there was in the game. He was a tremendous kicker, a reliable kicker. He just needed to get a kick to get some confidence. He was a good punter, too."

"Don was just a very, very consistent kicker," said Jerry Sherk. "You have to be something special to take over for Lou Groza and be successful. For most kickers, especially back in that day, they weren't looked at as part of the team because they didn't have the same aches and pains and go through the same grueling exercises to get in shape. But we really felt that Don was part of the team."

"Even though he was 'just' a kicker," according to Peticca, "to me he projected a toughness that he kind of relished the big kick that would determine the outcome of a game. I also remember, talking about his toughness, he was aggressive as far as once he kicked off or punted. He certainly went toward the play. He made a lot of tackles."

After retiring from the game, Cockroft, 79, worked in the oil packaging business, the oil and gas trade, and the mortgage profession. He has two grown daughters and a grown son. Cockroft eventually moved back to his old stomping grounds of Colorado. Several years before the move, however, he became an author, co-writing with Bob Moon a spectacular book about the 1980 Browns entitled *The 1980 Kardiac Kids – Our Untold Stories*. Cockroft interviewed every living player and coach from the 1980 Browns, plus others, including Art Modell, team physician John Bergfeld, trainers Leo Murphy and Bill Tessendorf, equipment manager Chuck Cusick, and various media members who covered the team.

"I believe it to be the most complete and comprehensive book on any team in any sport," Cockroft proudly stated.

Cockroft began the huge undertaking in 2008 when, while conducting an autograph session at the Pro Football Hall of Fame, an older woman approached him and said, "Sonny, why didn't you kick the field goal against the Raiders in 1981?"

"I said, 'Ma'am, that was 27 years ago … You know what? You're the millionth person who's asked me that question. I think I'll write a book about it."

What would have happened had Cockroft attempted that field goal 45 years ago?

"I've tried that kick hundreds of times in my mind," he said. "And every time, I make it."

19

BRIAN SIPE: KARDIAC KINGPIN

Quarterbacks chosen in the late stages of the NFL draft usually do not experience much success, let alone go on to a distinguished career.

Brian Sipe is an exception.

Sipe was a 13th-round draft choice of the Browns in 1972 out of San Diego State University. Although he set 11 Aztecs passing records and was the NCAA passing champ in 1971, scouts worried about his small frame (6-foot-1, 195 pounds). By the end of his NFL career, though, Sipe not only surprised the doubting Thomases, he also threw for still a team-record 23,713 yards in a playing career that lasted from 1974 to 1983.

Sipe was as cool as they come. Though he struggled his first few years and stumbled a bit towards the end, the prime of his career produced some thrilling moments. During that period, Sipe was at his best when the chips were down, when his team needed a lift late in the game. "He's a winner, and I think that just says it all in a whole," said Cleveland's all-time receptions leader Ozzie Newsome, a tight end for the Browns from 1978 to 1990, following the 1980 season in the NFL Films documentary *Kardiac Kids … Again*. "He does whatever he thinks it takes for us to win the game."

Remarked Reggie Rucker in the same documentary, also after the 1980 season, "Brian gets the football to the person that's open, and he probably reads defenses as well as anybody that I've ever played with, and I've played with Roger Staubach."

Sipe's talents, however, were questioned early in his career—due mainly to his size, and arm that was seen as too weak to compete at the professional level—and spent his first two seasons on the taxi squad. His attitude didn't help matters. He admitted his head was not totally in the game. "The first year I was in Cleveland I think I was more interested in having a good time than I was in impressing the coaches. … I was not 100 percent committed to making a career out of professional football," he revealed in the book *Sam, Sipe, & Company: The Story of the Cleveland Browns*. "I more or less figured it was an opportunity, that if somebody wanted to pay me to stick around."

"We didn't really know whether Brian wanted to play professional football or not," recalled Art Modell in the same book.

Sipe was such an unknown commodity that his name was spelled "Snipe" several times in the *Cleveland Plain Dealer* the day after the 1972 draft. He eventually got his act together and decided to seriously pursue the opportunity with the Browns. He finally made the regular squad in 1974. He actually gave Browns fans a glimpse of the excitement to come in a home game against the Denver Broncos that year. It was Browns fans' first taste of Sipe's late-game magic. With the Browns on their way to their first losing season in 18 years, Sipe saw action periodically in place of Mike Phipps. He came off the bench with the Browns trailing the Broncos, 21–9, late in the game. He immediately drove the Browns 79 yards to a touchdown, running the ball in himself from eight yards out. Then, with the help of a long punt return by Greg Pruitt, he scored the winning touchdown when he dove into the end zone from the 3 yard line as the Browns prevailed, 23–21.

Two years later, Sipe became the full-time starter when Phipps went down with a separated shoulder in the opening game. He had two decent years in 1976 and 1977 in which he began to blossom into a solid quarterback. "You could see that he had the attitude and work ethic," said Forrest Gregg, the Browns' head coach from 1975 to 1977. "He had everything it takes to be an NFL quarterback."

"Brian had very little physical ability but just had a tremendous feel for the game," said Jerry Sherk. "I don't remember him throwing any 60-yard passes, but he was kind of a master at taking what the defense gave him. He just had an intelligence, a savvy, and a knack for football and sports. I can remember playing racquetball with Brian, and I'd be ahead like 7–1, just dominating him. He was a guy who could just figure things out, and pretty soon I would lose like 21–12. And that's just the way he was. He could look at something and figure out where the weak points were and what his strength was and so forth."

"I think he had that mentality ... I don't think he feared failure. I think he enjoyed those situations," said Mike Peticca. "He had that undefinable gene that doesn't make a draft the be-all and end-all as far as projecting what a guy is going to be in any of the sports. I think it's just how he was made. It might be cliché, but I think he got all he could out of his physical abilities. He was so smart. One thing I remember about him is that you would ask him a question after a game or after a practice or whatever, and he would just talk. You could tell how much he just loved the game and the challenges it presented mentally and physically. He just really enjoyed talking about the ins and outs of the game. You could tell what a competitor he was."

"What I don't think Sipe gets enough credit for was his scrambling ability," said Michael Cuomo. "He made a lot of plays off script like the Monday night game against the Cowboys in '79 when he threw the long pass to Ozzie Newsome."

Sipe really hit his stride upon the arrival of Sam Rutigliano as head coach in 1978. Utilizing Rutigliano's pass-oriented offense, Sipe threw for 2,906 yards and 21 touchdowns that year. "Jim Shofner became the quarterbacks coach in '78, and Brian communicated very well with him," Doug Dieken said. "Brian was a very cerebral guy, and 'Shof' was a very cerebral guy and not too intense. There was just a chemistry there between the two of those guys that just made it work."

Sipe followed his solid 1978 season up with 3,793 passing yards and an NFL-high 28 touchdown passes in 1979. In the process, the Browns were becoming one of the NFL's most exciting teams, and were aptly nicknamed "Kardiac Kids" due to numerous victories (and some defeats, too) in the late going. However, Cleveland still missed the playoffs for the seventh straight year in 1979, finishing behind the always powerful Pittsburgh Steelers and the Houston Oilers in the AFC Central Division. Sipe's knack for pulling victories out of the hat continued into what became a magical 1980 season. In leading Cleveland to an 11–5 record and the Central Division title, Sipe was the NFL passing leader with a 91.4 rating and broke his own team record from the season before by passing for 4,132 yards. His 30 touchdown passes, tops in the AFC, broke Frank Ryan's team record of 29, set all the way back in 1966. Sipe also completed 60.8 percent of his passes (337 of 554). A major factor in the Browns getting over the Pittsburgh-Houston hump was the fact that Sipe was intercepted only 14 times after having tossed 26 the year before.

The awards that were bestowed upon Sipe made up a seemingly neverending list. Sipe was named the

NFL's Player of the Year by the Associated Press, Most Valuable Player by the Pro Football Writers Association of America and *The Sporting News*, Offensive Player of the Year by *Pro Football Weekly*, and AFC Most Valuable Player by United Press International.

Said Dieken, "For a guy who was a 13th-round draft pick to be the league MVP, that speaks volumes."

"You look at Sipe and you say, 'This guy can't be a quarterback,'" Thom Darden said. "His body was not a physique that would strike fear like a [Terry] Bradshaw, but Sipe had the mental strength and leadership qualities where, when things got tough, he focused even more. He was capable of finding the right spot to throw the ball most of the time. He was pretty sharp on where to get the ball and when to get it there. He couldn't run, but he had escap-ability. He was mentally tough. To me, that's the biggest thing. He didn't get scared, he didn't rattle. It looked like, especially in the huddle, that all the guys listened to him. You have to give him a lot of respect for that."

"His teammates loved him," Dan Coughlin said. "He had the guts of a burglar. He wasn't real big, but he had a heart. He was a hell of a leader. The players respected him so much. He made everybody around him a little bit better."

"I think Sipe's ability to shrug off failures was huge," said Mike McLain. "Let's face it, the guy threw a lot of interceptions in his career, but he was able to shake them off and just come up with gutsy plays when it was necessary. There was no fear in him. I just thought his resiliency to come back from mistakes was what carried him."

"I was talking with Brian one time about the Kardiac Kids seasons," said Sherk, "and he said, 'The reason we won all those games in the last few minutes was that the other teams would go into that terrible 'prevent' defense, and you just took what was there which was they would always allow passes underneath.' So he just gobbled up the field on short or medium passes. And he said, 'That's why we won those games.'"

Ironically, it was a miscue by Sipe that ended Cleveland's season that year. In an AFC divisional playoff game played in arctic-like conditions in Cleveland Stadium, the Browns lost 14–12 to the Oakland Raiders in heartbreaking fashion. Defeat was assured when a pass from Sipe was intercepted by Raiders strong safety Mike Davis in the Oakland end zone—the play was called "Red Right 88"—with less than a minute to go in the game.

In 1981 Sipe passed for nearly 4,000 yards, but his total of touchdown passes dropped to 17 while his interceptions sum skyrocketed to 25 as the Browns plummeted to a last-place finish. Sipe was benched after six games the next year in favor of third-year lefty Paul McDonald, who directed the team to two straight wins, enough to qualify the Browns for the expanded playoffs (and a quick exit) in the strike-shortened season despite a 4–5 record.

As the 1983 season approached, Sipe was determined to win his starting job back, and due to a strong preseason performance, did. "Paul McDonald is a very good quarterback," Sipe said, half smiling, towards the end of the '83 exhibition schedule in the NFL Films documentary *A Step Away.* "He's a very talented guy, and I respect him more than I'm around him. Someday, he'll be a very good quarterback in this league, but right now he still has a few things to learn from me."

The veteran backed up his words by passing for 3,566 yards in 1983, completing 58.7 percent of his passes, the second-highest completion percentage of his career. He threw an AFC-best 26 touchdown passes, but his 23 interceptions—and rumors of his exodus to the rival United States Football League (USFL)—were contributing factors to the Browns being the NFL's only 9–7 team (out of five) that year to miss the playoffs. Sipe did opt for the USFL, signing with Donald Trump's New Jersey Generals after the season. He left behind a legacy, though, that will linger in the minds of Browns fans forever.

Brian Sipe, 1979
Jerry Sherk/Wikimedia Commons

20

A DECADE OF DOUBLEHEADERS

When most sports fans think of the word *doubleheader*, baseball comes to mind for obvious reasons. But from 1962 to 1971, in Cleveland at least, a doubleheader not only meant two Indians games for the price of one but also two NFL games for the price of one. Soon after becoming the owner of the Browns, Art Modell came up with the idea to have two teams play a game followed by the Browns playing their only home game of the preseason against another team as a football doubleheader at Cleveland Municipal Stadium. The doubleheaders were all played on Saturday evenings except for the one in 1966 that was played on a Friday night. Every doubleheader except one drew at least 82,000 fans, the exception being the very first one that still attracted almost 78,000 fans.

"It was a stroke of genius by Modell," Dan Coughlin said. "Preseason attendance at Browns home games was 15,000, 18,000, 20,000, which was pretty typical for preseason games. People went to those doubleheader games just like they were regular-season games. It was a bonanza for the NFL because the Browns made money, the team they played made money, and the two other teams Modell brought in made more money than what they would've made normally."

"Regular-season games in the early '60s were not selling out in most of the venues," Steve King said. "So you get the preseason games, and they *really* aren't selling out. So Modell gets this idea that he can have his big stadium and his team, which was selling out all of its games, and they could bring two other teams in and make it a doubleheader, and they can split that pie four different ways. And it was no problem getting two other teams to come in because that section of the pie that they were getting was going to be bigger than anything they could get on their own no matter whose stadium they played in. It was a full house! You got to see two football games. Modell understood television, he understood marketing, and he was not afraid to take a chance. He volunteered his team in 1970 for the first *Monday Night Football* game when everyone else was running for cover: 'I'll not only volunteer my team to play, I'll host the game. I'm brave enough to host the game.' Off of that, who ever heard of a football doubleheader? The doubleheaders grew tremendously through the late '60s."

The following are the dates, results, and attendances of the preseason doubleheaders each season:

August 18, 1962 – Browns 33, Pittsburgh 10/Detroit 35, Dallas 24 (77,683)

August 17, 1963 – Baltimore 21, Browns 7/New York Giants 24, Detroit 21 (83,218)

September 5, 1964 – Browns 20, Green Bay 17/Detroit 24, New York Giants 10 (83,736)

September 4, 1965 – Green Bay 30, Browns 14/Detroit 25, New York Giants 21 (83,118)

August 26, 1966 – Baltimore 24, Browns 17/Minnesota 30, Washington 27 (83,418)

September 2, 1967 – Green Bay 30, Browns 21/Minnesota 16, Atlanta 3 (84,236)

September 7, 1968 – Green Bay 31, Browns 9/New York Jets 9, Detroit 6 (84,918)

August 30, 1969 – Green Bay 27, Browns 17/Chicago 23, Buffalo 16 (85,532)

September 5, 1970 – Minnesota 24, Browns 21/San Diego 38, St. Louis 27 (83,043)

September 4, 1971 – Browns 30, New York Giants 7/Pittsburgh 35, New York Jets 21 (82,710)

Recalled Jerry Sherk, "I think at least in one of the doubleheaders or maybe both of them I was a part of, I can remember we got to the stadium when the first game was going on, and a lot of us players would go down to the Indians dugout and just watch the game from there. We didn't actually walk out on the field because the fans probably would've cheered for us, and we didn't want to be a distraction. I thought it was pretty neat that there was a doubleheader, but I was more concerned about how I was going to play that night. I was just focused on my performance."

"I went to two doubleheaders, I think 1967 and '69," recalled Mike Peticca. "I just remember looking forward to being able to see four teams play. In those days, the top players *played* two-and-a-half, three quarters in preseason games. I remember, as a fan, just taking the exhibition games more seriously. Now they're a scam. Results mean nothing. I remember, as a kid they didn't count in the records or anything, but maybe the preseason games gave you some indication if there was any gap between the Browns and the Packers. I've never been a big fireworks guy, but the fireworks they had at those doubleheaders in between games, I think … I remember being impressed by those. I thought they were really good."

"I went to at least one doubleheader," Mike McLain said. "Preseason games are a joke now, but back then they were more of a game. It was a big deal. It was exciting. Going to the doubleheader was almost like going to one of those 'World Series of Rock' concerts back in the day."

"My first doubleheader in 1967 stands out as much

as anything because it was right before the last cut," Billy Andrews remembered. "I was a rookie and wasn't very highly regarded. Our center, Fred Hoaglin, had broken his hand and he couldn't snap the ball. The Browns didn't have a snapper. We were fixing to play the Packers, and I told the coaches I could snap. I wasn't expected to make the team. I thought we'd have seven linebackers, but that year they kept only five. The reason I was there was because I said I can snap punts, and they said, 'No, you can't.' And I said, 'I can.' They said, 'You're just sayin' that to make the team.' I said, 'Well, I want to make the team, but I can snap punts. I snapped them in high school and college, and I snapped more than 1,000 into a garbage can before I came here this year.' So they put a man over me in the Friday practice before the doubleheader. I snapped the ball right to Gary Collins. Then they said, 'Well, anybody can do it with no pads, no helmet, and nobody over you.' So they put me in the game, and my first snap was backed up on the 5 yard line with the bleachers behind me and more than 80,000 people there, and Ray Nitschke jumpin' in sayin', 'There's a rookie.' And I was about to faint. It was a moment that I will remember until I die. The snap went well, but then I went down to cover the punt and failed to tackle Herb Adderley, and he returned the punt for a touchdown. I thought I was going to get cut."

By the time 1970 came along, the doubleheader had grown enough that the other teams did not need to come in on the Browns' back end. "They were starting to be able to have preseason games that were well enough attended," said King.

The main reason the doubleheaders came to an end, however, was because Pat Modell, Art's wife, wanted her husband to become a little more cultured. "Pat wanted the Browns to play a game and then, instead of another game between two other teams, she wanted the Cleveland Orchestra to perform," recalled Dan Coughlin. "Art thought, 'Well, okay, if this is what Pat wants, we can do it for Pat.' So in 1972 that's what they were going to do, but right before the orchestra was about to hit its first overture, a storm to end all storms hit. Oh my god, did it ever come down. The orchestra never played that night, and they never tried it again."

21

FORREST GREGG: TASKMASTER

He wanted to give it a try. Forrest Gregg had never played football, but he thought it looked fun. His high school in the small town of Miller Grove, Texas, however, did not field a team at the time, in the late 1940s. The future Browns head coach, originally from Birthright, Texas, yearned to play the sport so badly, he not only transferred to Sulphur Springs High, about 40 minutes away, he actually resided in the school's gymnasium his entire sophomore year.

Yes, he lived in the school's gym.

"Not only did football look like something I'd like, I realized it was the only chance I had to get a college education," said Gregg, whose initial experience with the game actually came the year before when he played offensive and defensive tackle on the freshman team while still living at home in Miller Grove. "And my parents okayed me changing schools even though they stayed back on the farm. The superintendent eventually got me a place to stay at a lady's house in Sulphur Springs."

Gregg, who also played basketball and baseball at

Sulphur Springs, was a quick learner when it came to football.

"I started the first game my sophomore year against Paris High School, for whom [future Hall of Famer] Raymond Berry played, and Berry's father was the head coach," Gregg recalled. "It was an awesome game."

Gregg broke his arm during practice the next week and missed most of the season. He shined at tackle on both sides of the line for the Wildcats during his last two years, and soon realized he had a legitimate shot at getting a full ride to play in college. Schools including Southern Methodist, Texas A&M, Baylor, Houston, and Oklahoma State came calling his senior year. He chose Southern Methodist, the alma mater of his head coach at Sulphur Springs.

With the NCAA rule prohibiting freshmen from competing in varsity athletics in effect, Gregg mainly started at defensive end on SMU's freshman team in 1952. As a sophomore, he was a backup at offensive tackle and defensive end on a Mustangs team that finished 5–5.

"I played quite a bit," he said. "I got a lot of experience and a chance to play against a lot of great football players."

Gregg, who majored in physical education, was a starter at offensive tackle and defensive end during his junior and senior seasons. He then was chosen by the Green Bay Packers in the second round of the 1956 NFL draft. "I knew Green Bay played Detroit every year on Thanksgiving," Gregg said, "but I really didn't know where Green Bay was. All I knew was it was a long way from Birthright."

Gregg partook in the annual College All-Star Game in Chicago, a 26–0 loss to the defending NFL champion Browns before reporting to his first NFL training camp in the summer of '56. "That training camp was very informative," he said. "I learned a lot. I didn't start any of the five preseason games, but I got a chance to play a great deal."

This was pre–Vince Lombardi, as a gentleman by the name of Lisle Blackbourn was the Packers' head coach. The 6-foot-4, 249-pound Gregg, a backup at left offensive tackle when the regular season began, was eventually moved to right guard. He remained there as a starter the rest of the season as the Packers finished 4–8. He actually missed the final game of 1956 plus the entire 1957 season due to military obligations; he was drafted into the Army and was stationed in Fort Carson, Colorado.

Gregg returned to the Packers in 1958 under new head coach Ray McLean and was a part-time starter on offense at guard and tackle on a team that won just a single game. The next year was the beginning of what was to become a memorable decade in Cheesehead country. Lombardi, the New York Giants' offensive backfield coach the previous five years, came aboard as head coach and quickly turned the team's fortunes around, soon transforming the city of Green Bay into "Titletown."

"Before I went up to training camp in 1959," Gregg recalled, "I ran into a guy one day when I was in Dallas who'd played for Lombardi and he said, 'Do you know anything about Vince Lombardi?' I said, 'No, I don't. Do you?' He said, 'Yeah.' I said, 'Well, what do you know?' He said, 'He's a real bastard.'

"Lombardi was tough on us, very demanding. Expectations were to win, not just to play but to win. He pushed us hard. I really felt good about it because the two years I'd played in Green Bay I really wasn't conditioned [physically]. Under Lombardi, the team was well conditioned."

Gregg was the Packers' starting right offensive tackle from the very first preseason game in 1959, a season that saw the team finish 7–5, through the rest of his career in Green Bay. The next year, the Packers went 8–4 and won the Western Conference. They fell to the Eagles, though, 17–13, in Philadelphia in the NFL championship game, the first title game appearance for Green bay in 16 years.

"We were a young football team," said Gregg. "I don't think we realized just how difficult it was going to be, how tough it was to get to that title game and then win it."

Win it they did the next year, and then the next year, and then three more times before the 1960s came to a close.

"One of the games I remember most was that first championship victory [37–0] against the Giants in

1961," Gregg recalled. "That was important from the standpoint of … that was our first one. When I was in high school, we had good football teams, but we didn't win any championships. In college, we had good football teams, but we didn't win any championships. And up to that point in professional football, we'd had good teams but hadn't won any championships."

Gregg and the Packers repeated in 1962, beating the Giants again, 16–7. The 1963 Packers finished 11–2–1 but lost out on the Western Conference crown to the rival Chicago Bears, who finished a hair better at 11–1–2. The next year, the Packers slipped to 8–5–1 and in a tie for second place with the Minnesota Vikings. Green Bay returned to the title game in 1965 and defeated the defending champion Browns, 23–12, in a freezing Green Bay mud bath. Not only did the Packers become the first team since … the Packers (1929 to 1931) to win three consecutive NFL championships by beating the Dallas Cowboys in 1966 and 1967, they also won Super Bowls I and II, crushing Kansas City and Oakland, respectively.

The 1967 NFL title game victory over Dallas—known as the "Ice Bowl" in which Bart Starr scored with just seconds remaining to secure the 21–17 win—remains one of the coldest games in NFL history. Gregg remembered it like it was yesterday.

"I got a phone call at my apartment early the morning of the game from one of my teammates," he remembered. "He said, 'My car won't start.' I said, 'Why?' He said,

'You been outside yet?' I said, 'No, I haven't.' He said, 'It's 15 below zero [minus 48 with the wind chill].' I looked out the window and it looked like a nice, sunny day."

Boy, how looks can be deceiving.

"Later, at the stadium, before we came out to warm up," Gregg recalled, "I went out on the field to check the footing to see what kind of shoes to wear, regular cleats or basketball sneakers. I chose to wear my regular cleats. That's what we all wore. When you were out there trying to set your footing, you realized it was going to be an unusual day."

Lombardi left the Packers after the Super Bowl II triumph over the Raiders. Not surprisingly, the team's records the next three seasons dropped to 6–7–1, 8–6, and 6–8, respectively, under Phil Bengtson, Green Bay's defensive coordinator previously, a much more low-key coach than his predecessor. Gregg said that age was another reason for the drop-off.

"And I was one of those guys," he stated.

Gregg called it quits after the 1970 season, but it was a short retirement. He received a phone call from Tom Landry during the 1971 preseason while working a job selling sporting goods in Dallas. "The Cowboys had some injuries to their offensive line," Gregg said. "Tom asked me if I'd be interested in playing another year. I said yes right away. The team had been in the Super Bowl the year before, and I knew they had a great football team. It was a great opportunity for me."

Gregg was a backup offensive tackle and guard for a Cowboys team that returned to the Super Bowl and this time won it, defeating Don Shula's Miami Dolphins, 24–3. Gregg retired after the season, this time for good. He stayed in the game, though, catching on with the San Diego Chargers as their offensive line coach in 1972 and 1973, and then with the Browns as their O-line coach in 1974. The Chargers won just six games in Gregg's two years in Southern California, and the '74 Browns finished a franchise-worst (up to that point) 4–10.

Was it difficult for Gregg to coach clubs with miserable records after having played on teams that won five NFL titles and three Super Bowls?

"It was a learning process," he said. "I enjoyed coaching the offensive line. It's what I knew. I knew what made those guys tick."

In 1975 Art Modell promoted Gregg from offensive line coach to head coach, replacing the fired Nick Skorich. Gregg had a plan for how he was going to approach his new gig.

"I learned from Vince Lombardi and Tom Landry about football and about coaching, but we were also different in a lot of ways. I knew I couldn't be Lombardi. I knew I couldn't be Landry," he explained. "Even though I did take some things from those two men and applied them toward my coaching style, I thought I had to be myself if I was going to be successful."

Gregg considered himself to be a stern, demanding

coach for the most part. "This is a tough game," he said. "It's not an easy thing to do – play football and play winning football. It's a physical game, and if you're not prepared..."

"I was really fired up when Forrest took over as were a lot of players," said Jerry Sherk. "I was probably especially fired up because I knew about the Green Bay tradition. When I was in college right as I got drafted, I read Jerry Kramer's book *Instant Replay*, which talked about the Lombardi years and the Lombardi championships and the Lombardi method. And Forrest encompassed that. So when he took over, not that I didn't work hard in the offseason, I always worked hard, but I just thought, 'This is it. We're going to infuse Lombardi and Green Bay into Cleveland, and we're going to win championships.' I had my best years under Forrest. He pushed the team and got more out of the team than anyone could've expected with some talent that wasn't always top notch."

"Playing for Forrest," Doug Dieken said, "was like playing for Vince Lombardi because everything Forrest learned as a player in getting coached, he learned under Lombardi. And the success Lombardi had was pretty damn good, so why change it? Forrest was hard. He wanted physical practices. On the first day of practice, you did the nutcracker drill. That's not exactly tiptoeing into the season. Some guys didn't like the toughness that he brought. To be honest, I had no problem with it. I got along well with Forrest."

"Gregg instilled a toughness, which that team needed. He was a no-nonsense guy," Steve King said. "Skorich had kind of been lax, an older guy who kind of let things slide. Gregg came in and wanted to make the players tough, he wanted to run the ball and be tough on defense. They didn't have enough of an offense. He'd been an offensive tackle, but he had kind of a defensive mentality. He doesn't realize that Dave Logan is not a tight end. He can't get Mike Pruitt to become a productive player because of his hands. He wasn't that offensive-minded coach that would allow the team to compete with Pittsburgh and Cincinnati."

"I don't know why Modell went to Forrest Gregg other than he was a Packer," Dan Coughlin said. "In comes Forrest Gregg, a big, strong son of a bitch. Not a humorous bone in his body. Most of the players hated him. He's put them through terrible ordeals on the practice field. I'd put together an eating contest with a restaurant-owner friend of mine between a Browns offensive lineman and a Browns defensive lineman. Each side of the ball would pick a guy to be in the contest. The offense picked Barry Darrow, and the defense picked Mike St. Clair. So we had this big eating contest. The next day was the weekly meeting Hank Kozlowski from the *Lorain Morning Journal* and Bill Scholl from *The Cleveland Press* and I had with Forrest. There would always be lo-o-ong pauses, lo-o-ong silences in our conversations with Forrest because you didn't really have off-the-cuff conversations with him. He was not a good conversationalist. He never initiated a thought. To fill one of those voids, Scholl said to me, 'How'd that eating contest go last night?' I told him, 'Barry Darrow out-ate Mike St. Clair," and Forrest's ears perked up and his nostrils started to flare. His nostrils would *flare* in moments of stress and excitement. He said, 'Eating contest? Who cooked *that* up?' And I said, 'I did.' Who cooked that up? That was brilliant! And Forrest Gregg had no idea that that's what he said. Who cooked that up? I still laugh recalling that. The next day, Barry Darrow said to me in the locker room, 'He is going to put us through hell today.' And he did. It was a terrible practice for the players."

How concerned was Gregg after his first Browns team was creamed by Oakland, 38-17, on November 16, their ninth straight defeat to open the 1975 season? "If there's one thing I can say about that first team I coached in Cleveland, we didn't win but we didn't quit," he said. "And then, all of a sudden, we won a ballgame and then we won another one, and two weeks later we won another."

That '75 team finished 3–11. Then, in 1976, after a 1–3 start that included an injury to quarterback Mike Phipps that, for all intents and purposes, ended his season, the Browns, led by a 27-year-old backup by the name of Brian Sipe, won eight of nine games and actually had a remote shot at the playoffs heading into the final weekend. The team wound up 9–5 as Gregg won AFC Coach of the Year acclaim from the Associated Press.

With Phipps gone after a trade to the Bears, Sipe led the 1977 Browns to a 2–2 start against perhaps the toughest four-game stretch in NFL history—the Bengals (10–4 in '76), the Patriots (11–3 and a playoff berth), the Steelers (10–4 and a spot in the AFC title game), and the Raiders (13–1 and Super Bowl champs). They then proceeded to win three games in a row, capped off by a 44–7 trouncing of the Chiefs, and found themselves in first place in the AFC Central, regarded by many as the toughest division in the NFL. After that, the bottom fell out. They were beaten by the Bengals at home, then not only lost to the Steelers, but lost Sipe for the rest of the season to a separated left shoulder. The team won just a single game the rest of the way, finishing in the division basement at 6–8. Gregg was relieved of his duties with one game left in the season even though it was announced publicly as a resignation. For the rest of his life, he believed he was fired unfairly.

"I was hurt because I thought we were starting to establish something," he said. "We were getting better football players, the type of players who I felt we had to have to win. If Sipe had not been injured, I think we would've had a chance to make the playoffs. He'd been playing great football up to that point. I knew going into the season we were without a [capable] backup quarterback. And that was the reason we lost [in the second half of the season]. But in this business, it's win or else. Art Modell was the owner of the club, and he did what he thought was right for his team."

"When the team was 5–2 and in first place in Gregg's last season of '77, nobody is thinking that he's not going to be the coach by the end of the season," said King. "That's not even on the horizon."

"When we faltered as a team in the second half of that '77 season," Sherk said, "it felt like Forrest pushed us over a cliff, some kind of emotional cliff. Even though I could take it because I had the physical capabilities and I knew what I was doing, in the end he worked the team too hard."

"The front-office relationship with Forrest was collapsing," Coughlin said. "Bob Nussbaumer was a front-office guy. He'd hang around outside in Berea. There was a little theater area for the team to meet together. Nussbaumer was lurking outside the door trying to hear what Forrest was saying to the team. And Forrest heard that Nussbaumer was spying on him, so he casually walked over to the door. He threw the door open, caught Nussbaumer outside the door, grabbed him—Nussbaumer had been a pro wide receiver—pulled him into the meeting room, humiliated him in front of the whole team, and then threw him out."

After working in public relations for a Cleveland temporary agency for a year, Gregg in 1979 turned down several assistant coaching offers in the NFL.

"I wanted to be a head coach," he said.

He wound up traveling north to become the head coach of the Toronto Argonauts in the Canadian Football League (CFL). Gregg returned to the NFL in 1980 as head coach of the Bengals, a team that had fallen on hard times with consecutive 4–12 finishes. Gregg's first Bengals team improved to 6–10. The next year, 1981, was a dream season in the Queen City. Led by revived Ken Anderson, the Most Valuable Player of the league, Cincinnati won the AFC Central with a 12–4 record, won two home playoff games—including the "Freezer Bowl" against the Chargers in the AFC title game—and rallied from a huge deficit but fell short against the San Francisco 49ers in Super Bowl XVI.

"That was a good football team. We had good players," said Gregg. "It was also another chance for me to learn something as a coach. Paul Brown was there as owner and president who ran that club."

Gregg found it a bit strange returning to Cleveland to oppose the Browns, who still had several players who were there when he was the head coach. He had something in common with his new boss, Brown. They were both fired by Modell—Gregg in 1977, Brown in 1963. Asked if Browns week in Cincinnati was a big deal, Gregg chuckled.

"Let's just say that both of us were alert," he said.

Gregg acknowledged that he did feel great vindication in leading Modell's hated rival to the Super Bowl.

"I think Art was pretty well convinced that I was a good coach by then," he laughed.

The Bengals returned to the playoffs in the strike-shortened 1982 season but fell to 7–9 in 1983. Gregg resigned in order to accept the head coaching post in his old stomping grounds of Green Bay, vacated when his old Packers teammate Starr was fired. Gregg did not exactly set the world on fire in Titletown, going 25–37–1 in four seasons there. Included, though, was a rather satisfying upset of a playoff-bound Browns team in 1986, the Packers' first win that season in seven tries.

Gregg resigned after the 1987 season in order to become head coach of, and to revive, the program at another of his old stomping grounds—his alma mater, SMU. They had been issued the "death penalty" for the 1987 season by the NCAA for numerous rules violations. The school chose to sit out the 1988 season, too, when university officials determined it would be impossible to field a viable team. Although the Mustangs won just three games combined in 1989 and 1990 in a difficult situation to say the least, Gregg was thrilled to have coached at his alma mater.

"I really enjoyed coaching a bunch of kids who weren't the best football players in the world but didn't know it," he said.

Gregg was also SMU's athletic director from 1990 to 1993. He returned to the CFL as head coach of the Shreveport (Louisiana) Pirates in 1994 and 1995 as part of the league's brief attempt at expansion to the United States. He remained in the CFL and spent 1996 as general manager of the Ottawa Rough Riders, a franchise that folded after the season. Gregg then retired from football for good.

Gregg, whose son, Forrest Jr., took after his dad and played center at SMU, had quite a career in the NFL, especially as a player as evidenced by his seven first-team All-Pro selections and nine Pro Bowls. He was a first-ballot Pro Football Hall of Famer, inducted in 1977. He truly enjoyed his time in Cleveland.

"The fans there supported that team. They were loyal," he said. "And I made a lot of good friends there."

Gregg had no regrets.

"I got to do something I liked doing ... play football and coach football," he said.

In 2011 Gregg was diagnosed with Parkinson's disease, thought to be caused by numerous concussions from his playing days. He battled the beastly condition with all his might, and had a healthy outlook six years before he passed away on April 12, 2019, at age 85 when he said, "It's not fun, but I'm doing okay with it."

It was that same positive attitude Gregg put to use nearly 80 years ago in enduring his sophomore year in high school when he called the Sulphur Springs gymnasium home.

22

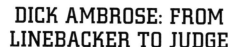

DICK AMBROSE: FROM LINEBACKER TO JUDGE

Dick Ambrose faced a number of big, strong, fast running backs during his nine-year career as a linebacker for the Browns. But going up against the likes of Franco Harris, O.J. Simpson, and even the bruising Earl Campbell didn't hold a candle to what Ambrose faced as a judge in the Cuyahoga County Court of Common Pleas, a position he held from 2004 to 2021.

Translation? Imposing the death penalty is a tad tougher than taking on the finest running backs the NFL has to offer. "I've had four death penalty cases already," Ambrose said in 2007, "and I have had to impose the death penalty in one situation already, and that's not an easy thing to do. I didn't lose sleep as much over Franco Harris as I do wrestling with the death penalty."

Ambrose's road to the bench was a little unusual. While practicing as a civil trial attorney with the Cleveland firm Nicola, Gudbranson & Cooper, LLC in the spring of 2004, Ambrose was contacted by the Cuyahoga County Court of Common Pleas. "One of the judges was retiring," Ambrose recalled, "because he felt he had no chance at winning reelection come November."

Thus, Ambrose left his position with the law firm—where he had spent the majority of his 17 years as an attorney—and accepted the opportunity bestowed upon him by the Court of Common Pleas. He joined the court in June 2004 and received rave reviews, but lost in the November 2004 election. He was fortunate, however, in that another judge happened to be leaving to pursue a career in the federal court system, so Ambrose remained on the bench. He finally won election—overwhelmingly, too—in November 2006. Ambrose, who presided over numerous civil and criminal trials, quickly earned a reputation as a hardworking and fair judge.

"The thing I enjoyed most is that I really felt like I could have an effect on people's lives and do good," he said. "We were to apply the law as it was written, but there was a human side as well, and you could be mindful of that while you were doing your job and interpreting the law and making sure it was applied properly. So I did enjoy that and being a part of hopefully a bigger picture of society."

In addition to his everyday duties as a judge, Ambrose was also a member of the Cuyahoga County Community Corrections Board, assisted with the court's Fugitive Safe Surrender Program, and was active with community groups seeking to educate individuals about their rights to seal a past criminal record so they could begin life anew without the stigma of a record.

Ambrose began his legal studies while still with the Browns, whom he played for from 1975 to 1983. He is a 1987 graduate of Cleveland Marshall College of Law. A 12th-round draft pick of the Browns in 1975 out of the University of Virginia where he majored in education, Ambrose was well aware of the fine tradition of the franchise.

"The only thing I really knew about Cleveland was the Cleveland Browns," he said. "I grew up in New Rochelle, New York, which is a suburb of New York City, and the Browns and Giants used to play at least twice every year. I'd go watch them play one another at Yankee Stadium, so it was a team I was familiar with. I became much *more* familiar when I got here about the depth of the tradition and the community's love for the team."

Hailing from a school such as Virginia—not exactly a football factory—Ambrose had grown accustomed to a losing atmosphere, as the Cavaliers posted 4–7 records each of his three seasons there. But even that did not prepare him for what he experienced as a rookie with the Browns—an 0–9 start.

"It was a very long season," he remembered. "For the most part, it was a team in disarray. We could never put anything together, and there was internal bickering amongst players and with coaches."

Ambrose saw action mainly on special teams early in the 1975 season but got his first start in Week 5 at Denver when middle linebacker Bob Babich went down with a knee injury. The coaches liked what they saw because, even when Babich returned, Ambrose stayed put in the middle while Babich was switched to the outside.

The adjustment from the college game to the pros was not exactly smooth sailing for Ambrose, but playing behind the likes of veteran linemen Jerry Sherk and Walter Johnson helped immensely.

"That was quite an impression," he said, "and I certainly looked up to those guys."

The 1975 Browns finished 3–11, but Ambrose helped the team rebound to a 9–5 record and the cusp of the playoffs the next year. The Browns fell to 6–8 in 1977, then Sam Rutigliano came aboard as head coach the next season and instilled excitement in the team by opening up the offense. Still, the Browns went 8–8 and 9–7 the next two seasons, landing them in third place in the AFC Central Division.

With the offense in full gear, the Browns realized that if they were to compete for the division title, the defense would need some tinkering. It started with a switch from the 4-3 alignment to the 3-4 by new defensive coordinator Marty Schottenheimer.

"The change took some adjusting," recalled Ambrose, who was positioned at right inside linebacker, where he mostly stayed the rest of his career. "We soon got the hang of it, though. Because you're not shielded as much [in the 3-4], you're facing a guard usually, the keys are a little bit different. I think it was overall good in retrospect only because we probably were a little stronger at linebacker than we were at defensive line back then, so we put the emphasis on a more mobile defense and one that didn't rely so much on defensive linemen to rush the passer. It got the linebackers more involved, and that actually turned out to be one of the strong points of Clay Matthews and Robert L. Jackson, who could both rush the passer very well, so that helped."

The Browns had high expectations for 1980, but two lethargic losses to open the season left fans shaking their heads. But not the Browns themselves, according to Ambrose.

"We had a good veteran group of players," he said. "We had gotten Calvin Hill from Washington, and we had Lyle [Alzado], and they added some stability and cohesiveness to the team. So the first two losses weren't necessarily going to be ones that would be considered a season loss at that point. We knew we could still recover, and we began to believe in ourselves as the season progressed."

Indeed, the Browns bounced back. They won 10 of their next 12 games—most of them in thrilling fashion—and were 10–4 and in first place. Ambrose said they had finally matured as a team. "I think," he said, "it was just playing together and knowing—especially when we had to, when it counted most—that somebody would always seem to come up with a big play."

Ambrose will never forget the scene at Cleveland

Hopkins International Airport when the team returned from Houston after upsetting Earl Campbell and the Houston Oilers in a battle for first place on Thanksgiving weekend. Upwards of 15,000 fans were at the gate to greet the new AFC Central leaders.

"It was unbelievable," he said, comparing the experience to being in a movie by Federico Fellini, an Italian director who was known for strange, expressionistic films filled with dream sequences and the like. "It really felt like walking into a dream. It must have been like 100 degrees from all the body heat. At one point we said, 'This is what it must be like to be the Beatles because people were running after us and stuff. They had to take us out [from] side doors, trying to get away from the crowd."

A win in Minnesota the next week would clinch a playoff berth for the Browns, their first in eight years. But Tommy Kramer's Hail Mary touchdown pass to Ahmad Rashad left the Browns in shock. Ambrose said the team stayed positive, though, entering the season finale at Cincinnati, where a win would give the Browns the division championship. The result was a hard-fought 27–24 victory over the Bengals.

Next came the infamous "Red Right 88" loss to Oakland in which Brian Sipe was intercepted in the Raiders' end zone late in the game. Ambrose was one of few observers who had no problem with the play call.

"I had confidence in our offense," he said, "and I

figured that if they called a pass, they would execute it properly or just throw the ball away. I know I heard Lyle say something like, 'I can't believe they're f-ing throwin' the ball!' And then I saw Mike Davis intercept the ball and hold *on* to it because I didn't think they could hold on to anything in that weather, and it just stuck in his hands and he held on to it. I couldn't believe it. All of a sudden, the place was dead quiet, the quietest I ever heard it. And I could hear them celebrating on the other sideline and still couldn't believe it."

Ambrose and the Browns fell flat on their faces in 1981 but rebounded the next two years, qualifying for the strike-shortened playoffs in 1982 (albeit with a 4–5 record) and barely missing a playoff spot in 1983 with a 9–7 mark. Ambrose's career came to a crashing halt during a victory over the New York Jets in Week 6 of '83 when he broke his leg. A comeback attempt during the 1985 preseason was put to rest when complications from the injury arose.

Upon retiring from the game, Ambrose, nicknamed "Bam-Bam" due to his hard-hitting style of play, had made quite a name for himself on the football field. He led the Browns in tackles every year from 1977 to 1981 and was the team's Most Valuable Defensive Player in '77. He was honored in 1981 by his teammates with the "Captain's Award," given to a team member who was "a worker, a team player, and an inspiration," which led to his co-captain status the next season.

"It might be cliché, but Ambrose kind of epitomized Cleveland," Mike Peticca said. "He obviously was very talented, but he also can maybe be put into the category of overachiever. I think he fit all those descriptions of the guy who got so much out of his ability. He was very smart, and he hit hard. He wasn't as good as some middle linebackers, but he was above average, just a shade below Pro Bowl caliber. Whatever aspects go into being a middle linebacker, I think he fit the prototype."

"Ambrose hit like a stone wall," said Steve King. "He played hard, he ran to the ball, had a nose for the ball. He understood what the linebacker was on the middle there, to make plays. He had brute force. He was really a tremendous player and never got the due that he deserved in that he really was as solid as there was of a linebacker in the middle in the AFC at that time. I really do believe that. He was good and was smart. He understood the game."

"In practice," Doug Dieken said, "you just hoped that he wasn't the guy you were supposed to block. Dick would stone you. That's how he got the nickname 'Bam-Bam.' He could light you up. He was a tough middle linebacker. He was solid."

"The Browns had so many good linebackers back then," Mike McLain said. "He was probably the least talented of them all, but he made the most out of what talent he had. His mental IQ probably helped him along the way."

Ambrose said he pondered a career in coaching but decided against it when he saw the countless hours coaches put in.

"The sad thing is," he admitted in 2007, "I probably ended up putting in almost as many hours [as a judge]. I'm usually bringing home work every night and just trying to keep up with the docket and make sure that things don't get too far behind because there's just so much stuff that comes down on a daily basis."

An inductee to the Cleveland Sports Hall of Fame, Ambrose, 71, was active in numerous community and professional groups, including the Cleveland Bar Association, the Make-A-Wish Foundation, and the Boys and Girls Club of Greater Cleveland. He also volunteered to coach linebackers for Bay High School for a few years.

Ambrose's playing days were a special time in his life and a special experience. "I'd like to be part of the resurgence of this whole area and see the Browns return to the prominence they once had in the '60s," he said. "I think if the Browns win their first four games, this place would be crazy. The whole town goes nuts."

Tackling his job with the Cuyahoga County Court of Common Pleas, said Ambrose, was aided greatly by his days of tackling opposing players.

"I think that actually being a defensive player was a help," he explained, "because I was used to things coming at me from a number of different ways—pass, run, linemen cracking down on you, receivers cracking back—all that kind of stuff, just a flurry of activity. It was kind of the same way as a judge. We were trying to handle multiple cases at the same time, so you had to bounce around a lot, go from thing to thing and then try and just keep things moving along as fast as possible.

"I think you learn things over the course of your life that you don't forget, and you get ahead with hard work, and you basically try to out-prepare the other guy."

When he was a judge, no longer did Ambrose have an opponent per se like his playing days or even when he was an attorney.

"You still had to be prepared, though," he said, "and that was always the mantra of any good player."

One thing the former judge could have done without in his position was the penning of his signature on a seemingly never-ending basis.

"I probably signed my name more then," he laughed, "than I ever did as a player for autographs."

23

SAM RUTIGLIANO AND THE KARDIAC KIDS

When the New Orleans Saints lost to the Tampa Bay Buccaneers in the Louisiana Superdome on December 11, 1977, the Saints' wide receivers coach, a guy by the name of Sam Rutigliano, was bummed out—big time. The 46-year-old Rutigliano was convinced that his first—and possibly only—shot at becoming an NFL head coach had been shattered, tossed unceremoniously into the nearby Gulf of Mexico. Before the game, Rutigliano had received a phone call from longtime friend Peter Hadhazy, the general manager of the Browns.

"Peter told me, 'We fired Forrest Gregg [as head coach]," Rutigliano said. "'Dick Modzelewski's going to be interim coach, but I'm telling you right now, if you don't blow the interview, you've got the job.'"

Rutigliano was convinced the Saints' 33–14 loss to the Buccaneers crushed his chances of becoming the Browns' fifth full-time head coach.

"We'd just lost to a second-year expansion team that had lost its first 26 games," he said. "I said to my wife,

Barbara, 'I'm not gonna get that job now, for crying out loud.' I figured it was over."

Boy, was Rutigliano ever wrong. Not only were his chances not "over," they were as hot as the Cajun food the Bayou is known for.

"I get a call from Hadhazy midweek before our last game in Atlanta," he said. "He says, 'Everything's on. We'll have a flight to Cleveland for you sometime Monday.'"

Even so, Rutigliano still did not think he had any chance at getting the job. "I just figured we [the Saints] had such a lousy team," he said, "and then we go out and lose to a team that had lost 26 games in a row."

Rutigliano's three-day interview with the Browns, however, put him in better spirits.

"I really felt good about it," he said.

On the Browns' plane ride home from a season-ending loss in Seattle—with defensive coordinator Dick Modzelewski as the interim head coach—Reggie Rucker, a wide receiver for the team at the time, approached team owner Art Modell and said, "The guy you want is Sam Rutigliano." Rucker had Rutigliano as his position coach for a year and offensive coordinator for two years in during Rucker's three seasons with New England from 1971 to 1973. A few days later, on Christmas Eve, the phone rang in Rutigliano's Covington, Louisiana home. It was Modell who said, "I want to speak to the new head coach of the Cleveland Browns."

Not a bad present from St. Nick! The hiring was made official four days later.

"It was a lifelong dream come true," Rutigliano said.

Like most coaching "lifers," it was a long and winding road to his position as the Browns' boss man. As in 19 moves, 13 homes, and 23 different schools for his three children. Officially, though, the road began when he was born in Brooklyn, New York, on July 1, 1931 (ironically, the same birthday as historic Cleveland Stadium, where Rutigliano would begin waving his magic wand some 47 years later).

He attended and played receiver and defensive back at Erasmus Hall High School, the oldest high school in America and an institution that produced such stars from the sports world as Al Davis, Jerry Reinsdorf, Billy Cunningham, and one-time New York football Giants part owner Bob Tisch, plus entertainers Neil Diamond and Barbra Streisand.

Rutigliano and his Warriors teammates won the New York City championship in his junior year, 1949. During his senior year, an New York City coaching strike ended up cancelling the season.

"I could have stayed and graduated from Erasmus," Sam said, "but I wanted to play football to get a scholarship."

Rutigliano had already accepted a full ride to the University of Tennessee.

"A guy named Jay Albrecht," he said, "who had

graduated from Erasmus a few years before me ... he was also kind of a recruiter. He set it up for me to attend East Central Junior College in Decatur, Mississippi. I started as a receiver and defensive back, and also played basketball and ran track for East Central while attending the high school across the street."

In the spring of 1951, Rutigliano left for Knoxville, Tennessee.

"I was a full scholarship kid ... living in a dorm," he said, "with an assistant coach taking me to night school at a local high school so I could graduate."

Things worked a little differently back then.

He wound up getting redshirted in 1951 in case the NCAA found out he had played for the junior college in Mississippi. He never actually suited up for a game as a Volunteer, transferring to Tulsa University the next year because he felt he had a better chance of playing there. He was redshirted again, then started two years as a receiver and safety for the Golden Hurricanes before graduating with a physical education major in 1956.

"I wasn't good enough to play in the NFL," he said, "but I could've played in the Canadian Football League. I had injured my ACL at Tulsa, though, and I'd married Barbara my senior year, so I pretty much was wanting to get started with a career."

Rutigliano returned to his old stomping grounds of Brooklyn, and got his first of many teaching positions— and the head coaching job—at Lafayette High School while studying for his master's degree in education at Columbia University, which he completed in 1958. His teams at Lafayette were successful, but he was not happy with the direction that high school football in "The Big Apple" was headed, so he took the head coaching job at Greenwich (Connecticut) High School.

His teams did well there, too.

Rutigliano then took a job as director of physical education, athletic director, and head football coach at Horace Greeley High School in Chappaqua, New York.

"It didn't go very well there," he said. "I decided then that I really liked teaching, but I knew if I stayed in Chappaqua the rest of my career, I'd eventually have to give up the coaching because of the directorship and the athletic director's job.

"All I could think about was three o'clock."

Rutigliano's aspiration at the time was to become a college football coach, and he got his start as defensive backs coach at the University of Connecticut. Former Browns linebacker Lou Saban was the Terrapins' head coach, and future Detroit Lions head coach Rick Forzano and legend-in-the-making Lou Holtz were on the staff. After two years at UConn, Rutigliano took a job as the quarterbacks/receivers coach at the University of Maryland in 1966. After the '66 season, he received his "big break."

"Saban was offered a 10-year contract as general manager and head coach of the Denver Broncos," he recalled.

Saban took the offer, and brought Rutigliano with him. Rutigliano was the Broncos' receivers coach for four years, and Denver did not fare too well, but Rutigliano was slowly gaining experience at the professional level. He then spent three years—two as offensive coordinator, one as receivers coach—with the Patriots, another team struggling big time. However, he got the opportunity to coach Jim Plunkett, the 1970 Heisman Trophy winner from Stanford and 1971's number one overall draft pick. Rutigliano's long-range goal at the time was simple.

"I wanted to be an NFL head coach," he declared.

Foxborough, Massachusetts, is where Rutigliano first met Rucker. Later in the decade, the two of them would join forces to help bring incredible excitement to fans on the North Coast.

After his stint with the Patriots, Rutigliano made a career move that few coaches do. With his entire NFL coaching background having come on the offensive side of the ball, Sam decided to broaden his skills by taking a job as the New York Jets' secondary coach. He spent 1974 and 1975 on the "Gang Green" staff, coaching alongside a guy by the name of Buddy Ryan, the Jets' linebackers coach.

"It was a tremendous experience," Sam said. "Later on, when I became head coach of the Browns, you have no idea how much having experience coaching on both sides of the ball helps you."

Rutigliano also said that "Broadway Joe" Namath was anything *but* Broadway.

"Joe was totally immobile ... totally immobile," he said. "But once he came to camp, he worked harder than anybody. He was just great. I used to tell our defensive backs how fortunate we were to go every Wednesday, Thursday, and Friday in 7-on-7 and 11-on-11 against Joe Namath. How else could we have been better prepared to play the quarterbacks who we had to play every game?"

In 1976 Rutigliano received an offer to return to the University of Connecticut as head coach.

"I said to my wife, 'I want to be a head coach in the NFL, but it's just not working. I'll take the job at Connecticut. We'll buy a place on Cape Cod. I can win there. It's not what I really want, but...' She said to me, 'You mean to tell me after all these sacrifices, you're going to give up now?'

"That's all I needed."

Rutigliano decided then and there he was going to continue full force with his aspiration to become an NFL head coach. He joined Hank Stram and the Saints in 1976, and spent two seasons there. "In the two years I was there," he said, "Archie Manning played in 10 games because of a bicep tear."

Rutigliano said Peyton and Eli's father was better than both of his sons.

"Archie just played on rotten teams, that's all," he said. "He ran for his life his entire career. If you put

Archie on those Steelers teams of the '70s, he'd have accomplished the same thing Terry Bradshaw did."

The first thing Rutigliano did upon his hiring as Browns head coach? Get on the telephone.

"I called every single player on the roster," he said. "The first one I called, obviously, was Brian Sipe."

Well, actually, the *very* first thing Sam did was contact three guys who he had befriended in the past and who knew a little bit about the quarterback position—future Hall of Famers Len Dawson, Bob Griese, and Fran Tarkenton.

"I said to each of them, 'Tell me what you think about Brian Sipe,'" he said. "They all talked about 'the indefinable *it* that everybody talks about, 'the intangible.' And they also said, 'Brian has great accuracy and is a leader.' But nobody knew it!

"Both Modell and Hadhazy had said publicly, 'Sipe's not the guy.'"

Rutigliano got Sipe on the phone. "Brian said to me, 'Listen, Coach. My arm is sufficient," Rutigliano said. "'I just need to have more smart guys around me.'"

The new coach then called Rucker. "He asked me if I'd be willing to forgo any personal goals," Rucker recalled. "He said if nobody cared who got the credit, we'd have success. I told him, 'I'm with you.' And he said, 'Well, okay, we'll do this together.'"

Rutigliano said phoning each player helped him tremendously—and helped the players, too.

"And that's how it all started," he said. "Every one of those players always mentions, 'Coach called me on the phone personally.' I just wanted to kind of communicate with them."

Communication. Rutigliano was a master at it—with his coaches, the media, the front office, and especially his players.

"It was very important for me to be able to communicate with my players and make that connection," he said. "The key to making that connection is all about communication. Teaching [in school] helped me a lot—to be able to draw pictures, to be able to tell compelling stories."

"If you talked to Sam, he would mention Blanton Collier a lot," Steve King said. "Collier was a tremendous communicator, and that's what Sam did. He understood how to reach people, he understood how to inspire and motivate people, he understood how to talk to the media. He had an air of confidence."

"Sam was such a charming guy. The players seemed to like him. He was the perfect guy to replace the dour sourpuss Forrest Gregg," Dan Coughlin said. "He loved to put the ball in the air, whereas Gregg wanted to run the old Packer offense, which was give it to Hornung and give it to Taylor, and he had neither Hornung or Taylor. Sam was a breath of fresh air."

"I just loved Sam," said Michael Cuomo. "I remember the media used to beat the piss out of him because he didn't wear a headset during the games. They kind of made it seem like he wasn't really coaching the game. But he was fine. He was a good man. He was a players' coach obviously. He was the right coach for that team. They were a swashbuckling team, and he was the head of it."

Added Doug Dieken, "Sam was a fun guy to play for."

Rutigliano cited a moment in the locker room after an excruciating loss to the Steelers in his first season of 1978.

"We were undefeated, and they were undefeated," he said, "and we got screwed on the first play of overtime and lost the game. So I took the moment and said to the players, 'Look, let's capture the moment. Now, listen to me because I'm only gonna talk for about two or three minutes. This is the best team in the world! And I want you to know that there are gonna be 10 or 12 [players on that Steelers team] who are gonna be enshrined in Canton, Ohio, about 25 years from now. Let's be able to understand what you did against this kind of a team.'"

"Sam was the first coach I ever dealt with who knew both sides of the ball," Thom Darden said. "He had coached all the different positions, so he could watch us practice and tell us what we were doing wrong. And you knew he knew what he was talking about. Most coaches couldn't do that, so I respected him a lot for that. And Sam always had a quip. He was quick-witted, so he always had something to say in a situation that required him to say something. He'd make you laugh, make you think."

Rutigliano said his 11 years as an assistant with four NFL teams were beneficial to say the least.

"Doing it around guys like Stram, Saban, and Weeb Ewbank, I learned a lot," he said. "I kept a diary of all the different things that I *wasn't* going to do and the different things that I *would* do if I ever became a head coach."

Rutigliano's first NFL draft with the Browns was akin to pocketing a quick million on one's first trip to Las Vegas. The team had two first-round picks; they chose Clay Matthews with the first and Ozzie Newsome with the second.

Talk about hitting the jackpot.

Newsome was intelligent. So were the speedy Rucker and the sure-handed Logan, plus Greg and Mike Pruitt, and veteran newcomer Calvin Hill. Add to that a stellar offensive line led by veterans Tom DeLeone, Robert E. Jackson, and Doug Dieken [whom Rutigliano coached in the Senior Bowl when "Diek" was at Illinois], and Rutigliano had a pretty good offense to work with. The defense was not exceptional but, led by a strong linebacking core, was a hard-hitting unit.

"Greg Pruitt could catch the ball as well as any back in the league," said Rucker. "Mike Pruitt couldn't catch the ball naturally, but he worked hard at it and became a really successful receiver out of the backfield. And you've got Calvin Hill, who could catch the ball. So you've got explosiveness there. And you've got Sipe, a born leader."

"Sam understood offense," said King. "The Browns

became as close as they'd been to the teams of the Blanton Collier era when Sam came. There was a lot of offense. They were moving the ball and throwing the ball downfield. It was a prolific passing attack. Sam understood where the game was going with the passing attack. He made things fun."

Rutigliano's first Browns team got off to a surprisingly fine start, winning its first three games. The "Kardiac Kids" were born the next year, in 1979, but they were conceived during that '78 season. There were several down-to-the-wire finishes that resulted in an 8–8 record. One of them was a week two sudden-death win over the Bengals in Cleveland Stadium in which the Browns rallied from a 10–0 halftime deficit.

"Things weren't going very well offensively," Rutigliano said. "About midway through the third quarter, Brian came up to me and said, 'Coach, I... ' I said, 'Look, don't even ask me. You're ... my ... quarterback. You're gonna be the quarterback. I want you to know that that's the decision that's already been made. I believe in you.' And then he got us in position to kick the winning field goal, and we won the game."

Rutigliano reiterated that connecting with people is key, but doing it at critical times—like he did with Sipe against the Bengals—was crucial.

"You can encourage them and let them know, 'Hey, listen buddy, you don't have to worry,'" he said. "I could see the way Brian connected with his teammates. He gets the crap beat out of him, his helmet's almost turned around, and he goes back in the huddle and he says, 'My fault, guys, my fault.' The players loved him.

"Brian Sipe empowered everyone around him, including special teams, including the defense, and certainly the offense, to play at a level they never dreamed they could play at."

Rutigliano had a special way of encouraging his men.

"Each player is different," he said. "You have to kind of know where that button is for each guy. I really believe that."

"Forrest Gregg didn't know what he was doing," Rucker said. "The man couldn't get it done."

Rutigliano's philosophy, on the other hand, was simple—air it out and go for it. He preferred the spread-the-ball concept on offense. His '79 Browns team won three thrillers to begin the season, cementing their "Kardiac Kids" image.

"Gregg didn't know how to throw the football," said Rucker.

The fact that the Browns won the '79 season opener against the Jets in New York proves that anything is possible, that miracles do indeed occur. The Browns were out of it, had no shot, were dead. That is why they called them the "Kardiac Kids," though – because they *weren't* out of it, *did* have a shot, *weren't* dead.

Trailing, 22–19, and pinned on their own 16 yard line with 31 seconds to go in the game and no timeouts left,

Sipe hit Logan for a 14-yard gain to the Browns' 30-yard line. After two incompletions, Sipe hung a prayer down the left sideline that the tall, lanky Logan miraculously grabbed after bobbling the ball with nothing but green jerseys around him as he was heading out of bounds at the New York 33 yard line with eight seconds left. As Don Cockroft lined up for a 50-yard field goal attempt, a late flag was thrown and Jets defensive end Mark Gastineau was called for roughing the passer. That put the ball on the 18 yard line and thus made Cockroft's field goal try much easier from 35 yards out. Cockroft split the uprights with five seconds left, tying the score at 22 and forcing overtime.

Right cornerback Oliver Davis intercepted a Matt Robinson pass late in sudden death and returned the ball 34 yards to the Jets' 31 yard line. A 21-yard strike from Sipe to—who else?—Logan put the ball on the 10 yard line. The Browns didn't waste any time getting Cockroft back on the field. His 27-yard field goal with 15 seconds left gave them a remarkable 25–22 victory, sending 48,472 fans at Shea Stadium home in disbelief.

In the Browns' fourth game of the season, they stunned the nation by routing the also unbeaten Dallas Cowboys—"America's Team"—in front of a rocking Cleveland Stadium on *Monday Night Football* to improve to 4–0. The Browns were in such a "zone" that night, they scored 20 points before Tom Landry's crew could manage a single first down. It was a memorable evening, one that Cleveland fans had been dreaming of for a long time.

Doug Dieken will never forget that magnificent evening in which former President Gerald Ford paid a visit to the Browns locker room after the game to congratulate the team, especially fellow University of Michigan alum and player Thom Darden, who intercepted a Staubach pass and returned the ball 39 yards for a touchdown.

"Nobody, I don't think, counted on us having a chance, and we were able to pull it out," Dieken said. "That was a big game. It was kind of one of those that gives you the ability to get some confidence with what you can do. You get a win like that and start getting confidence, and all of a sudden you start having some success.

"It was exciting football. We'd be down a couple touchdowns at halftime, and Sipe would tell the offensive coordinator, Jim Shofner, 'Hey, we've got 'em right where we want 'em,' and Brian or whoever would find a way to make the plays that made it happen. It wasn't just one guy; it was one of those situations where everybody did their part, it was different people making different big plays every week. And we had a lot of success, we won a lot of games in the closing minutes. It was good team chemistry, and sometimes that will win you some games but sometimes they'll slip through the cracks."

"That night was so special," Rutigliano said, "because Art Modell had invented *Monday Night Football*, and we played very well that night. The crowd, the Monday night, the Dallas Cowboys, Tom Landry ... Lou Groza said to me the next day in Berea, 'Boy, what a great feeling that must've been for you.' I said, 'It's inexplainable. It's inexplainable.'

"I would go into Art's office after every home game, win or lose. Obviously, it was always better when you won. But after that Dallas game, he was just ... if we could have stopped right there, we would have both walked into the Hall of Fame in Canton, Ohio. It was great. I really cherish the moment."

"To me," added King, "Sam bordered on genius in terms of what he did in a short period of time. He completely changed the climate of the team."

Rutigliano and the Browns were brought back to earth by losing three straight games. They then won three straight—two in electrifying fashion—but then were upset at home by Seattle. Next came perhaps the most memorable Kardiac victory of the season—a 30-24 sudden-death triumph over the Miami Dolphins at Cleveland Stadium in which the Browns trailed, 24–17, late in the game. Everyone—players and coaches—has an "I really am in the NFL" moment.

This was Rutigliano's.

"Miami had the number one defense in the NFL," he said. "And that Saturday night the Browns' all-time team—all the famous players [except Jim Brown]—came back and gathered at a hotel on the west side of town and were also at the game. Dante Lavelli, Lou Groza, Otto Graham … and I'm there saying to myself, 'This can't be true, this can't be true.' Here I was a kid watching these guys play, and now I'm here shaking hands with them, and I'm the head coach of the Cleveland Browns! It was a great moment."

Rutigliano said that although all the players contributed, Sipe was the straw that stirred the drink in all of the Kardiac victories. He compared Sipe to the greatest clutch player in another sport's history.

"Michael Jordan. Sixth game. NBA finals [in 1998]. The Bulls are down by one point [to Utah]. Less than 10 seconds to go," he said. "Four guys have grapefruits in their esophagus. Not Michael. He hit the game-winner. Brian had that same crave-the-moment 'it' factor about him. A lot of guys tell you that a quarterback is like a tea bag … you know … a lot of them get in hot water. But Brian craved the moment. He loved it, he absolutely loved it."

"We just developed a mentality," Logan explained, "where it's a mindset that a team gets —and I can speak of this offensively—where we just knew that we were never going to be out of a game. We always felt like we could hang around, and even if we were behind, we could come back. That's something teams can build on, and I think we did that. It all just fell into place for us."

The '79 Browns lost their last two games and barely missed the playoffs with a 9–7 record. Rutigliano, though, was still named United Press International's AFC Coach of the Year. The 1980 team lost its first two games but rebounded in Kardiac fashion by winning 11 of its last 14—many with late-game comebacks—to dethrone the two-time defending Super Bowl champion Steelers and win the AFC Central Division title.

"We got off to a great start in 1979 but were a team that didn't know how to finish the season," Newsome said. "You have to realize '79 led to 1980. We learned how to finish in 1980. We tasted some success in '78, and in '79 we didn't know how to handle the success, I guess you could say. And then in '80 we did. We were a confident team; we were a confident bunch. At that point, we felt like once we got out on the field, we could do it."

Rutigliano was not afraid to rock the boat. "When he brought in Joe DeLamielleure in 1980, that ticked off the whole rest of the offensive line," said King. "And Sam, while he respected what those guys thought, didn't care. He thought they needed another bolstering in the middle of the line. DeLamielleure took Robert E. Jackson's job, and the players hated that, but Sam knew what he wanted."

Rutigliano was simply mesmerized by the thousands and thousands of fans who greeted the team at Hopkins Airport after a Thanksgiving weekend upset of the Houston Oilers in the Astrodome propelled the Browns into first place. He was even more mesmerized by the thousands and thousands more who greeted the team at what is now the IX Center—there was too much damage done to the actual airport after the Houston game to try it again—after the division-clinching win in Cincinnati four days before Christmas.

"Mayor Voinovich was there!" Rutigliano exclaimed. "It was … it was unbelievable! It was absolutely unbelievable."

"Sam was the best," said Mike McLain. "I took over the Browns beat during the 1980 season for the rest of the year when Jim Swearingen, our beat guy, got sick. I remember looking out the window after returning from the win in Cincinnati feeling I was on a plane with the Beatles because there were so many people there. Well, Sam and I were the only two people left on the plane, and he came up to me and asked me, 'Are you coming to Berea tomorrow?' I said, 'Yeah.' He said, 'Come to my office. I have a game ball I want to give to Jim.' And I just thought, 'This is Sam's crowning moment as the Cleveland Browns coach, and he's thinking of an ailing sportswriter to give a ball to.' That pretty much says it all about Sam. I'll always remember that."

"I think Sam was a genuine nice person who cared about people," Mike Peticca said. "His Inner Circle drug rehabilitation program in his later years as Browns head coach demonstrates what his character really is, how he genuinely likes people. The impression I got was that he probably treated the clubhouse guys and the people who served food during training camp the same as he did the team's star quarterback. I think he was very real. And, if you were a media person, that translated into making it an easy team to root for. He was creative in his coaching both tactically and relating to players."

Rutigliano was named AFC Coach of the Year by UPI for the second straight season.

Every longtime Browns fan knows what happened next. The infamous "Red Right 88" loss to the Oakland Raiders in mind-numbing cold weather—as in a wind chill of 37 below zero.

"The field was a sheet of ice," Sam said. "I've never been more respectful of football players than I was that day with what they had to go through. I mean, there were icicles in their noses."

As for the "Red Right 88" play in which Sipe was intercepted by Mike Davis in the Raiders end zone with less than a minute to go in the game?

"Brian just threw a bad pass, that's all."

"Football is supposed to be fun," said King. "This is not brain surgery; we're not splitting the atom or finding a cure for cancer. We're not looking to solve world peace. It's supposed to be fun, entertaining. And those teams, the 'Kardiac Kids,' I'll never see a team that was as fun as them. That was as good as it gets. It was just so much fun to watch those guys."

The playoff loss to Oakland seemed to deflate the "Kardiac Kids." The 1981 Browns did a 180, slipping to 5–11 and last place.

"We had some injuries to some key players,"

Rutigliano said, "but we just weren't the same team. We lost close games that we won in 1980."

The 1982 Browns started well, but finished 4–5 in the strike-shortened season that saw Sipe get benched in favor of Paul McDonald in week seven. The Browns lost a first-round playoff game to the Los Angeles Raiders.

Sipe was back as the starter in 1983, and the Browns looked to be headed back to the playoffs with an 8–5 record in early December. They lost two of their last three games, though, to finish as the only one of five 9–7 teams to miss the playoffs.

With Sipe off to the "greener" pastures of the United States Football League, McDonald had the quarterback job all to himself in 1984. The season was a disaster as a 1–8 start ended in a 5–11 record and a new head coach. Rutigliano was replaced at midseason by defensive coordinator Marty Schottenheimer. "Just the fact that he lasted six-and-a-half years really says something because that's probably double the norm," said Peticca. "And, given what the Browns' history was, there might've been more pressure to win in Cleveland than lots of places. I think the fact that Modell stuck with him through eight games in the '84 season in which there were a lot of close, tough losses was an indication that everyone had an affection for Sam.

"One thing I remember is that after the last day of the draft every year, Sam would come down to the area at Baldwin-Wallace where the media guys were, order pizza, and sit around with the media guys and just shoot the breeze."

Rutigliano received a head coaching offer from the Buffalo Bills and interviewed with the Houston Oilers, but instead chose to call it quits. A part-time position he had held with NBC television in the mid-1970s, during which he sat alone in a booth during postseason games—including Super Bowls IX and XI—and anticipated what was going to happen on the next play, then told the producers, who in turn informed the announcers, led to his return to the network as a game analyst for four years, from 1985 to 1988.

"It was great," he said. "You got paid, and you didn't have to win."

In '88 Sam also became an author, co-writing his autobiography with Bert Akin entitled *Pressure*. The next year, he decided to return to coaching and accepted the head job at Liberty University, at the time a Division I-AA school, in Lynchburg, Virginia. He spent 11 years there, leading the Flames to six winning seasons, including a 9–2 mark in 1997. After stepping down from the Liberty job, Rutigliano continued coaching overseas in NFL Europe from 2000 to 2006 for three different teams as an assistant under former Boston College head coach Jack Bicknell. He also conducted Italy's first-ever American football clinics for several years after leaving the Browns. In addition, he was a Browns analyst for WKYC Channel 3 and Sportstime Ohio.

Ever since arriving in Cleveland, Rutigliano had involved himself in community affairs to the utmost. He and Barbara have two grown daughters and a grown son plus several grandchildren.

Some two weeks prior to getting fired by Modell in 1984—following a disheartening home loss to New England in which a play call he made late in the game likely cost his team a victory—Rutigliano said to the press, "I'm good for Cleveland." He was mocked and ridiculed by many for that remark. That's what losing will do.

But, as usual, he was correct. The time may indeed have come for a coaching change, true. Sam Rutigliano, though, *was* good for Cleveland.

And still is.

Sam Rutigliano, 1979
Jerry Sherk/Wikimedia Commons

Printed in the United States
by Baker & Taylor Publisher Services